HYGGE

THE DANISH WAY
TO SIMPLER, HAPPIER LIFE

DISCOVER SECRETS TO MANAGING A FAST
LIFESTYLE AND INTRODUCE UNENDING
HAPPINESS TO YOUR HOME WITH ART OF HYGGE.

By: Alexander Parker

TABLE OF CONTENTS

Introduction

In today's world where everything seems to be rushed, confusing, and polarizing, when was the last time you have taken a break to reflect upon this question: "Am I happy?"

If you could not say for certain that you are happy with the way you are living your life right now, know that you are not alone. A lot of people feel like they are going through each day on auto-pilot.

Aside from this lack of connection with the present, many also feel isolated from the people they care about. Days when they could spend the whole afternoon chatting, playing, or just simply dining together are rare and far in between.

Though several people feel this way and live in this manner, it does not mean that you have to settle for this kind of lifestyle, too. You are allowed to seek your personal happiness, comfort, and security, even if doing so would put other things in your life to the sidelines. You also do not have to just imagine what it would be like to be free from your worries, doubts, and insecurity.

Several so-called lifestyle gurus have long recognized this growing epidemic of discontentment and unhappiness among the current generation. They have recommended various ways to address such issues, but why gamble with your happiness by relying on the advice of a few when you can tap into the wisdom of the Danish people?

This book is written to guide people through the process of slowing things down in order to, once again, appreciate and enjoy the simple pleasures found within the home, at work, and while spending time with family and friends. Through this book, you would be able to understand what hygge truly means, and how you can apply this to your life in easy and doable ways, all year round.

By carefully compiling the best ideas from various studies, discussions, books, and articles about hygge, the author of this book offers an effective solution for the dreary way of living that many people burdened themselves with. Whether you want to learn how to relieve yourself from the various stressors in your life, or you wish to improve upon your relationships with your loved ones, this book will show you how adding a bit of hygge into your life could make a meaningful and lasting difference.

Sounds too good to be true?

The people of Denmark would beg to differ. For decades now, they have consistently proven that their hyggelig way of living enables them to reach and maintain their status as one of the happiest people in the world. Their satisfaction with the quality of their lives ranks among the highest even when compared to other well-developed and thriving nations. Given this, it is no wonder that hygge has become one of Denmark's greatest treasures and "exports" throughout the world.

You might be wondering why hygge is not considered a universal practice at this point. It has already exhibited exceptional results that are both attainable and sustainable.

The answer lies in the intangibility of the concept itself. Some people who do not take the time to understand hygge believe that a few candles, a cardigan, and a fur throw would be enough to make their lives hyggelig. That superficial assumption could not be more wrong.

Hygge is immaterial. It is a feeling that touches upon so many values in life. As such, there is no single word in any language that fully captures its true essence. Seeing a picture of a hyggelig room in your social media feed, therefore, would not likely be enough for you to understand what this way of living means.

Fortunately for you and everyone who wants to understand hygge, this book tackles on all the important topics that you need to learn in order to gain a comprehensive and practical mastery about this Danish concept. Filled with examples, tips, and discussions, this book covers the following points:

- History, Definition and Impacts of Hygge
  Discover the origins and meanings of hygge, how it has affected the world in significant ways, and other cultural concepts that bear some similarities with it.

- Benefits that You May Expect by Practicing Hygge Like a Danish
  Motivate yourself to fully embrace hygge by learning of its benefits for your body, mind, spirit, and relationships.

- Easy Ways to Apply Hyggelig Principles at Home
  Find out how you can turn a house into a home that feels joyful, warm, and comfortable for yourself, your family, and your guests.

- The Best Hyggelig Recipes that You Should Definitely Try
  Enjoy good food and warm drinks by serving extremely hyggelig dishes to your loved ones.

- Effective Parenting Strategies Based on the Core Values of Hygge

Raise your kids into well-rounded, open-minded, and empathic individuals by instilling the practice and values of hygge to their young minds.

- Turning the Workplace into a Hyggelig Space
  Bring the comforts of a home into the workplace in order to increase productivity, enhance creativity, and promote cooperation among the employees.

- Fun and Exciting Ways to Practice Hygge All Year Long
  Learn the various ways and fun activities that could make you feel hyggelig no matter how cold the season is.

- How Hygge Leads to a Frugal Lifestyle
  Understand how hygge can help you save money in different aspects of your life.

As you go through each of these points, you will begin to see your life, and the world in general, in a more positive light. At some point, you will begin noticing things that you used to take for granted. By the end of it, you will feel a deeper connection with your true self, with your environment, and with everyone around you.

The Danes have shown the world that hygge can make these things possible. Now, you will be armed with the knowledge on how they have managed to do so. Each page of this book holds the secrets of unlocking a hyggelig way of living for yourself. Do not worry about the changes that you would go through along the way towards a happier and cozier life. This book is designed to make this transition as easy and simple as possible—much like the kind of pace that hygge wants you to follow.

Everyone is highly encouraged to read this book and embrace the concept of hygge. No matter how riddled with anxiety, depression, or other negative emotions you are right now, learning how to apply hygge in whichever manner you prefer would lift up spirits in wondrous ways.

To make your reading experience more immersive, find a cozy spot where you could read this book with little to no distractions. Pour yourself a cup of your favorite hot beverage, and light up a couple of scented candles around you. Once you have set the perfect scene, grab this book, crawl under the softest blanket that you have, and begin your journey towards hyggelig enlightenment.

Chapter 1

Everything You Need to Know About the History, Meaning, and Impacts of Hygge

You have picked this book to read because you want to turn your life around, or elevate the quality of your life through hygge. But before delving into the whys and the hows, do you know what "hygge living" exactly mean? Are you familiar about its foundational values and principles?

Many people apply hygge by simply following the example of other people. They think they want to do it as well, so they emulate the practices of others without really knowing the reason behind the act. The problem with this is the possibility of being disillusioned about the benefits of adopting hygge as a way of life. You would only be touching it on a superficial level, thus the positive outcomes that you may be expecting would most likely materialize on a lesser scale.

To truly enjoy the hygge life, learning its definitions, history, and impacts on societies and the world in general should be the first step that you must take.

Understanding the Definitions of Hygge Living

Hygge encompasses a lot of things so it could not be sufficiently described in a single word in the English language. A good way to understand its meaning is by learning the core values and principles of hygge—comfort, companionship, relaxation, connection to nature, simplicity, and authenticity.

- Comfort

   Practicing hygge means seeking comfort in various aspects of your life. When one achieves this, you would be able to move forward while feeling happy and contented with the choices that you have made along the way. Following this path could then eventually lead you to discovering the meaning of your life.

   How is this possible?

   In hygge, comfort is all about coziness. When you feel cozy, everything within you and around you feels right. For instance:

   o Feeling comfortable with yourself means that your focus is in the here and now rather than the past or the future. You genuinely like yourself, thereby allowing you to move with confidence and a sense of purpose.

You express positivity in the things you say and do. Through this, you are able remain level-headed and relaxed, even when faced with challenges in your life.

Nothing could stop you from going after your dreams and aspirations in life. You are strongly connected with your thoughts, feelings, and spirituality, thus giving you a good starting point about the path that you should take.

o Spending time with other people is a critical component of a hygge-based lifestyle. As such, you have to learn how to feel comfortable with those around you. Doing so would then enable you to build close relationships that are beneficial to everyone involved.

Being comfortable while in the presence of other people can be achieved even when you have a naturally reserved personality. Experts in hygge believe that this all starts with establishing good eye contact with the person you are interacting with. This non-verbal gesture sends out a message that you are self-assured, regardless of how you truly feel inside.

At first, it may feel uncomfortable, but through regular practice, you would be able to maintain eye contact without much effort from your part. Just remember to avoid staring too much at other people because you would likely make them feel uncomfortable.

Inspiring comfort among those around you is considered as another social aspect of a hygge lifestyle. Your self-confidence draws people towards you. Observing how you speak and act tends to bring out the best in everyone around you. Ultimately, your positive outlook in life influences others to take on the same practice.

o If you think you are safe and secured in your environment, then you can say that you feel comfortable to be in it. You can stay there without fear of being harmed, and without being agitated by the little things around you.

There are certain points in life wherein you would not be able to feel totally comfortable in your surroundings right away. Moving to a new home, visiting a foreign city, taking on a new job—these scenarios require a certain period of time to adjust and regain the sense of comfort you have towards your environment.

Still, hygge requires you to move past this adjustment period so that you can continually live this kind of lifestyle. Later on, you will learn in this book how to apply the principles of hygge in order to feel comfortable, once more, with your environment.

Achieving comfort in everything you do can take a lot of time and effort. However, as many practitioners of hygge could attest, this initiative is worth given its numerous benefits for you and the people you care about.

- Companionship

Hygge is all about supporting one another on the path towards happiness. Making a habit out of being helpful rather than being self-centered could bring forth a more meaningful life, and more joyful experiences for everyone.

No one can go through life all on their own. Throughout your lifetime, you would connect with different people to varying degrees. Some would end up being your close friends and mentors, while others would come into your life once but never to be seen again. Many people are going to interact with you, regardless of their overall impact on you. Therefore, try to make the most out of your moment together with them.

Feeling the warmth of companionship with the people dear to you and with the people who would come and go in your life gives you more than just joyful experiences. It is also going to touch you on a spiritual level. The things you could learn from them would allow you to grow in ways that you will not be able to do so on your own.

For example, random acts of kindness, especially those by performed by strangers, is a good source of such lessons. By witnessing or experiencing this for yourself, you would be able to learn the value of paying it forward. Being kind to someone right now—without needing something in return right away—would give you a chance to feel the joy of receiving help from unexpected sources. However, the true essence of companionship, in terms of hygge, pertains to the act of extending help to others out of your own will—with or without benefiting you.

Hygge does not also discount the fact that there are certain issues in life that you would have to face alone in order to learn and grow from them. Resolving your own problems without relying on others is a commendable act. Asking for help from others, however, does not lessen its significance. Life can tough as it is, so why make it harder by ignoring or refusing the help that other people could give you?

Companionship in hygge means loving and caring for others unconditionally. It does not ask or want, but it gives willingly and wholeheartedly. Through this, you will create a strong sense of togetherness that promotes growth and development within everyone involved.

- Relaxation

Nowadays, almost everyone finds themselves rushing through the day without ever taking a pause to appreciate their experiences and the things around them. If you always have something to worry about, or something that needs to be accomplished at the soonest time possible, then you are likely one of these people.

Hygge, however, promotes mindfulness and the true value of time. Yes, you have to think about the important things in your life, but that does not mean that you have to constantly force yourself to finish everything in record time.

Find the time to take it slow, even at least once or twice a day. You can do so by making it a point to savor your first cup of coffee for the day. Staying a little longer in the bath before going to bed can also be a great practice of hygge. Take your time in enjoying these simple things because you might end up regretting not doing so later on.

- Connection to Nature

  Though hygge is normally associated with things that you can do inside your home, it also touches on the sights, sounds, aromas, and experiences that you can enjoy from nature. You may be able to appreciate these by simple, relaxing engagements such as going out for a walk in the park, reading your favorite book under the shade of a tree, or keeping yourself hydrated at the beach by drinking coconut juice straight from the shell.

  You can also connect with nature by getting your blood pumping through exciting activities, like playing football out in the sun, skiing in the mountains, or swimming in the sea.

  Winter might take away most of the greeneries, but that does not mean that you will not get to practice hygge. Keeping and tending to some potted plants in your home would enable you to appreciate the simple delights that nature has to offer.

- Simplicity

  Hygge covers the simple things in life. Studies show that the Danes tend to place a lesser value on materials and luxuries in comparison to others. What they treasure more are their personal experiences and their relationships with family members and friends.

This kind of thinking enables them to live a simple life that costs a lot cheaper than hoarding things or keeping up with rapidly changing trends in fashion, technology, among others. For instance, going out on a hike with your close friends can be an excellent opportunity to create lasting memories that would also promote a better appreciation and connection with the environment.

Quiet moments like relaxing by the fireside with cup of hot chocolate are also considered as hygge because simple self-care measures are just as important as caring for others.

- Authenticity

    In hygge, placing a great value on comfort, relaxation, and simplicity does not mean that you have to take shortcuts whenever you go. Rather, you should aim for authenticity in everything you do.

    Take for example the matter of indulging yourself with your favorite comfort food. Eating it would bring you joy, but you could get a lot more from the experience by trying to create it from scratch.

Fortunately, most of the popular comfort foods are quite easy to prepare, thus making it easier for you to learn how to do so. To get you started on this, chapter ____ of this book provides several delightful hygge recipes that you should definitely try making yourself.

You may take this to the next level by getting yourself onboard with the farm-to-table trend. Skip the supermarket, and head instead to the local farmers' market. Better yet, try planting and tending to a few herbs and small plants in your home so that you can harvest your own ingredients.

Hygge means choosing authenticity over convenience, whenever applicable. Aside from the satisfaction of laboring over something that matters to you, doing so would enable to take better care of your body in the long run.

All in all, hygge is about improving one's quality of life by establishing and maintain a good relationship with the self, with other people, and with the environment.

Considering these definitions of hygge, it should no longer surprise you that its practitioners, particularly the Danes, are regarded as the happiest people in the world. But how did hygge come into existence in the first place? Where did it all start, and how did it become one of the most popular lifestyle trends across the globe?

To answer these questions and more, here is a quick overview of the history of hygge and its impacts on modern society and world in general.

Discovering the History of Hygge

The pronunciation of hygge is not the only confounding aspect of the word. Experts have tried to trace its roots, but up until now, no consensus has been reached aside from the fact that the concept appeared first sometime in the 19th century. Here are some of the common speculations about the origins of hygge:

- "hyggja"
    - Source Language: Old Norse
    - Meaning: "to think"

- "hugr" or "hug"
    - Source Language: Old Norse
    - Meaning: "mind", "consciousness", "mood" or "soul"

- "hugge"
  - Source Language: Unknown, but most likely Old Norse
  - Meaning: "to embrace"

- "hygga"
  - Source Language: Old Norse
  - Meaning: "to comfort"

- "hycgan"
  - Source Language: Old English
  - Meaning: "to consider" or "to think"

These terms appeared in 19th century Danish literature, but they were culturally relevant in the Scandinavian countries. At the time, Denmark had been reeling from its loss in the Second Prussian War that took away the duchies of Holstein and Schleswig from them. As a result, the Danes began suffering from a significant financial decline.

In response to this economic downturn, the nation rallied behind the idea of regaining what has been lost by rebuilding from within. Their focus shifted to growing their communities and fostering their relationships with one another instead of interacting with other nations.

The strategy has proven to be quite effective since it gradually elevated Denmark, along with its Scandinavian neighbors, as the happiest and wealthiest nations in the world. As such, the practice of hygge piques the interest of other societies that are experiencing massive shifts in their culture, politics, and economies.

Appreciating the Various Impacts of Hygge Across Different Societies in the World

The concept of hygge has been in existence since the early 1800's, but it was only in mid-2010's that the rest of the world caught wind of it. This rise in popularity continues to surge across different platforms—blogs, social media, magazines, and books—thus enabling hygge to transcend the barriers imposed by language and geography.

Case in point, the term itself was included in some "Word of Year" lists in 2016. This uptrend in its usage most likely stems from the dozens of books and articles that have been published particularly in the US and the UK. Several lifestyle experts raved about it that, in 2017, Pinterest recognized hygge as one of the hottest décor trends among its users. Up to this day, people in Twitter and Instagram continue to post hygge-related images, and to discuss what makes something hygge.

Proponents of a lifestyle based on hygge did not find this phenomenon surprising, given that its core qualities revolve around the pursuit of comfort and happiness. Its entry into the mainstream consciousness of several countries reflect the shift of interest towards what is happening within their nations rather than what is going on outside their borders.

This trend can be observed playing out in a major scale in the US and the UK. The Republican campaign during the US presidential election of 2016 centered around the idea of making their country "great again" by prioritizing nationalistic interests rather than establishing and maintaining global partnerships. Meanwhile, in the UK, majority of the citizens have voted on a referendum that would separate UK from the European Union.

Given these major political upheavals, how does hygge influence the lifestyle of the people living during these uncertain times?

At the most basic level, hygge promotes happiness and togetherness. Pursuing these values enable individuals to gain the strength and willpower to overcome the challenges that come their way. Furthermore, they would able be able to offer support and encouragement to those around them, thus creating a sense of belongingness that could stand the blows of the unexpected changes in life that lie beyond one's control.

The impacts of hygge also extends beyond the self, home, and community. It could also significantly alter the way people work for a living. Though it may sound counterintuitive for societies that promote active competition, practicing hygge at work means aiming for optimal work-life balance. Rather worry about promotions and paychecks, the focus should be on building good working relationships with one another, and enhancing the working environment into becoming a relaxing and conducive space for thinking and creativity.

As the world continues to debate on whether nationalism or globalism is the future, the concept of hygge persists and widens its scope of influence among individuals who are seeking for happiness and comfort in their own little ways.

Having learned the definitions, history, and impacts of hygge, you might be thinking that the concept is not entirely unique. After all, it is natural for humans to seek for solace and happiness in their life. Your own culture might also have its version of a hygge-like lifestyle. Here are some examples of the popular concepts that bear great similarities with the meaning, origins, or applications of hygge.

- Fika

  Pronunciation: FEE-kah

  Many consider this as one of the core practices of the Swedes. Essentially, this is Swedish version of a coffee break. It involves relaxing refreshments and delightful snacks, combined with feelings of contentment.

  Fika is largely based on the perception on work and break times in Sweden. The people there believe that one should not work more than what is required. Taking a break at different points of the day is not considered a waste of time. Rather, it is viewed as a means of maintaining a healthy balance in one's life.

  Through this, you would be able to moderate your life well. You would be able to practice self-care and connect with your family and friends, while ensuring a satisfactory performance at work.

  To practice fika, set aside some time every day to hang out with the people you like and care about. Look for a quiet and relaxing place where you could catch up with them over coffee and pastries.

As you can tell by now, fika and hygge promotes the idea of slowing down and appreciating the positive vibes brought about by the presence of other people. Both concepts want you to live in the moment, and enjoy the simple things in life.

- Friluftsliv

Pronunciation: free-LOOFTS-leev

This Norwegian term, which literally means "free air life", pertains to the act of connecting with nature by participating in various outdoor activities, such as skiing, sledding, hiking or even simply walking or running around the park. Norway, after all, is home to several nature spots that millions of locals and tourists visit each year.

However, frilutsliv is not just about spending time outdoors. It is a way of living, much like hygge. This concept encourages people to practice mindfulness to be one with nature. Ultimately, frilutsliv would enable you to reach a higher level of consciousness, and to establish a stronger connection with your spirituality.

How do Norwegians practice this kind of lifestyle?

First, they make it a point to teach the concept to children. Beyond the home and the school, children are frequently given the chance to apply frilutsliv so that they would continue to do throughout their lifetime.

You do not have to live or stay in Norway just to do so as well. You may practice frilutsliv anywhere you are, as long as you learn how to properly appreciate the time you spend out in nature. This does not mean that you have to schedule a hike in the mountains, or go skiing every weekend. Simple acts, such as taking a deep breath of fresh air while you are out on a walk, would enable you to feel in touch with the world around you.

Friluftliv does not mean that you have to do everything alone so that you can better connect with nature. You may also embrace it along with your family and friends. Feel free to participate in group outdoor activities—just make sure to be mindful of the things that you are doing with your companions.

When you spend time at the beach, set aside a bit of time to enjoy the warmth of the sun on your skin, breathe in the sea breeze, and feel the sand under your feet. Doing so would relax your body, calm your mind, and lift your spirits.

- Gemütlichkeit

Pronunciation: guh-MYOOT-lik-kayt

Much like hygge, the German concept of gemutlichkeit refers to feeling warmth and comfort while in the company of other people. It may be practiced inside the home, while at work, or during social events. However, unlike year-round hygge living, this mostly applies during the winter months only.

Experts believe that the harsh cold outside had driven the Germans to create a warm and comfortable atmosphere wherever they are staying. For instance, hanging out with the people you have dined with is considered as gemutlichkeit, as long as everyone is having a grand time. So does playing a classical piano piece while your loved ones listen and drink tea. In this sense, you may say that gemutlichkeit is all about spending quality time in a cozy environment with the people you care about.

Introverts may also enjoy practicing this concept by doing your favorite pastimes. Reading your favorite book by the fireside, or immersing yourself with a thousand-piece puzzle and a glass of wine would produce the ideal atmosphere that gemutlichkeit is promoting.

- Gezelligheid

  Pronunciation: geh-zehl-LEEG-hayd

  Considered as the Dutch version of hygge, the concept of gezelligheid places great importance on a spending time with your family, friends, and loved ones in a relaxing and cozy setting. It is also a year-round lifestyle, thereby encouraging you to experience it wherever you go.

  To better understand this way of living, here are some examples of gezelligheid in action during different seasons of the year:

  - Spring
    - Having a picnic at the local park
    - Going on a fishing trip

  - Summer
    - Hanging out at the beach
    - Playing outdoor field sports, such as football and Frisbee

  - Fall
    - Taking a stroll at a park to appreciate the colors of fall
    - Arranging intimate get-togethers

- Winter
  - Snuggling with your loved one under a fleece blanket
  - Attending a choral performance

- Koselig

Pronunciation: KOO-suh-lee

This Norwegian concept of coziness shares more similarities with hygge compared to friluftsliv. Basically, koselig means to experience a warm and joyful time with your family and friends. Furthermore, much like hygge, koselig has no limitations when it comes to its applications due to its broad meaning.

Koselig may be exhibited through the food you prepare, the sweater you choose to wear, the way you decorate your home, and the plans you make for the weekend. Even just the way you converse with your family and friends may reflect the koselig principle when you do it in a way that would build lasting friendships and impart good vibes.

No matter what season it is, koselig can be practiced with relative ease. Good weather comes and goes, so it is important to make the most of it. Even when the weather becomes wet, cold, or dreary, Norwegians try to turn keep things light, warm, and positive.

Those living in tropic regions might think that koselig is just for those who experience harsh winters. That assumption is not true because at its core, koselig is about developing a deep appreciation of the people and the things around you. Therefore, you can create it wherever you are as long as you have the right mindset for it.

Humans naturally crave for anything that would make them feel happy and contented. Hygge, as well as other similar concepts, can be regarded as effective means of fulfilling this need.

Moreover, switching into a lifestyle that is centered on hygge would give you a chance to improve the overall quality of your life. The next chapter discusses the numerous benefits that you can enjoy through hygge living.

Chapter 2

Understanding Why You Should Pursue Happiness Like a Danish

Numerous studies conducted about the level of happiness exhibited by the Danish people have shown that they owe much of it from their practice of hygge. The attribution of joy, warmth, and comfort to this kind of lifestyle have lead many people to believe that it would also turn their life around.

But how exactly so?

Though arguably the most well-known benefit of a hyggelig lifestyle is getting to enjoy the simple pleasures in life with your loved ones, there are plenty of other benefits that you may expect from taking the initiative to apply its principles to various aspects of your day to day living.

To better understand and appreciate the effects of hygge on a personal level, here are the top physical, mental, and emotional benefits of adopting this kind of lifestyle:

- For the Body

Hygge promotes feelings of safety and calm. When sustained for a reasonable period of time, this kind of environment enables the body to adjust accordingly. Rather than being always geared up for moments of stress and danger, the body would be able to relax and refocus its resources on it others functions, such as healing, self-cleansing, and fighting off bacteria and viruses.

Upon achieving this bodily state, you would be able to reap the following physical benefits of hygge:

  o Lower Levels of Stress Hormone

    The human body is hardwired to react accordingly to various types of danger. Back in ancient times, this mechanism enabled the survival of mankind against predators and harmful forces of danger. Such threats did not completely disappear over time, but rather they evolved in ways that significantly affect one's day to day living.

    For example, everyone goes through the hassle of meeting the demands from different aspects of life—taking care of the family, tackling a heavy workload, or looming due dates for bills. Though these stressors are quite different from fending off wild beasts, the body recognizes these as threats to one's life.

When this happens, the body releases cortisol, the main stress hormone, and adrenaline into the blood stream. This would then result to:

- Elevated heart rate
- Increased blood pressure
- Higher level of glucose in the blood
- Altered immune system
- Suppressed digestive system, reproductive system, and cellular growth

These changes in the body allow a person to have more energy for movement and brain function. More bodily resources are also allocated for the repair of cells and tissues. Ultimately, the stress hormones promote functions that could aid in a fight-or flight situation, and repress those that do not contribute much or at all.

Once the stressor has been eliminated or minimized, the effects of cortisol and adrenaline also dissipate until the body has been restored to its normal functioning. However, many people do not get to de-stress themselves long enough for the cool down to happen.

Extended exposure to stress hormones tend to be highly disruptive towards almost every important bodily function. As such, it would put anyone at serious risk of developing:

- Various cardiovascular diseases
- Weight gain
- Mental impairments
- Digestive problems
- Inability to sleep
- Depression
- Anxiety
- Severe headaches

Given these probable effects of overexposure to stress hormones, it is important to learn how to cope with stressors in a healthy manner.

The practice of hygge is considered as one of the more effective ways of doing so. At its core, this type of lifestyle promotes the idea of removing one's self from situations that could be emotionally overwhelming, and instead, focusing on the things that could make one happy.

These principles are quite easy to apply than you might think. Compared to other lifestyle trends, hygge does not require much effort or money. In fact, the less you spend, the more hyggelig your life would be. Examples of hyggelig moments that could significantly reduce the amount of stress hormones include but are not limited to:

- Sitting beside a fireplace
- Baking cookies, cakes, and other types of pastries
- Having an intimate dinner with family and friends
- Snuggling under a thick blanket with your loved one
- Wearing a cozy cardigan
- Going on a nature hike

Essentially, hygge is all about being kind to yourself, to the people around you, and to the environment. Appreciating the simple pleasures in life is a good way of giving your body enough time to recuperate from the effects of stress hormones.

o Better Quality of Sleep

Sleep plays an important role in achieving good physical, mental, and emotional wellbeing. During this period, the body could rest and repair itself. Growth and development also gets a boost, especially among children.

The right amount of sleep varies per age group, but on an average, a seven-hour sleep could do wonders for the body. Failing to reach the prescribed amount could lead to sleep deprivation, which in turn affects the following:

- Vulnerability towards illnesses, such as heart disease, stroke, hypertension, and diabetes
- Memory and concentration
- Control over mood and emotions
- Performance while awake
- Personal safety

Getting the number right is critical, but insufficient if you have attained it through artificial means, like taking sleeping pills, or if you woke feeling tired after a restless sleep. The quality of your sleep matters just as much as the number of hours you have slept.

Health experts recommend different strategies to attain enough good-quality sleep. For example:

- Establishing and following a ritual before going to bed
- Keeping the same sleep schedule every day, regardless if it is a weekday or the weekends
- Refraining from using any electronic device at least one hour before bedtime

These strategies have proven to be effective for many people. Hygge, however, boosts the expected outcome from taking on any or all of these initiatives. It can also make it easier for you to create a long-lasting habit out of these sleep-inducing behaviors.

Applying hygge to the way you sleep is quite simple to do. For many, it starts by turning the bedroom into a relaxing sleep sanctuary. Anything that could make both your body and mind feel at rest may be placed somewhere in this space—fluffy pillows, knitted blankets, or scented candles. Having these items in the bedroom could help trigger the regular release of serotonin, the primary hormone that is linked to a restful night.

Once the ideal setting has been achieved, hyggelig practices could form part of your regular sleeping ritual to further relax the body and the mind. Here are some of the highly recommended activities that you should definitely consider:

- Taking a nice, long hot bath
- Listening to relaxing music
- Performing meditation or mindfulness exercises
- Writing down the things you are thankful for in a daily journal

Take note, however, that hygge does not provide a complete guarantee that it would resolve the sleeping problems that you have, such as insomnia or sleep paralysis. At best, it could help you create an environment that would increase your chances of getting the ideal duration and quality of sleep for you. For more serious and persistent sleep-related problems, you should seek the advice of a medical expert.

o Improved Weight Management

Hygge is not a diet plan nor is it a weight loss measure. What it does for weight management is enhance the way you eat, sleep exercise, and entertain yourself. It would not make you shed ten pounds right off the bat, but practicing hygge will help you keep your body in good shape. For instance:

- Being mindful of what you eat and drink

  Taking the time to savor and appreciate every bite and sip will help you regulate your eating habits. Rather than making do with frozen meals and fast food items—both of which contain high levels of sodium and trans-fat— you would be more conscious of the things you consume every day.

  Furthermore, chewing the food slowly would lengthen your eating time. According to experts, doing so would make you feel full even if you have not yet eaten a significant amount of food.

- Turning the act of eating into a special occasion

  Due to the numerous demands of modern life, some people might be tempted to eat a quick meal in front of the TV rather than cooking and sharing meals with the people you care about.

Hygge promotes social experiences that are special for everyone involved. It is not just about eating good food. It also encourages the use of good music, an engaging atmosphere, and nice conversations with the people eating along with you. Through this, you would be able to have an easier time in switching towards a healthier diet that could be filling for both your tummy and your heart.

- Making your favorite food rewards for accomplishments and good performance

Completely depriving yourself of special treats, such as chocolate truffles or special types of cheese, could be counterproductive when it comes to weight management. Preventing yourself from eating certain foods would increase your desire to have it, which then leads to overeating.

Indulging yourself from time to time and in moderation is extremely hyggelig. Eating your favorite food is a pleasant experience that could put a nice ending to a particularly busy but productive day.

- Exercising the body outdoors

  A study conducted among more than 800 adults by the Peninsula College of Medicine and Dentistry has concluded that there is a significant correlation between exercising outdoors and energy levels. The more they exercise outside, the more revitalized they feel afterwards.

  Getting an extra boost of energy after a workout would help in maintaining a regular exercise routine. The returns exceed your efforts, thus inspiring you to do more.

- Getting the right amount of high-quality sleep every day

  Sleep deprivation has been linked to obesity primarily because of the imbalance in hormones that it causes. Adopting a hyggelig lifestyle could prevent you from suffering from this condition since it recommends various ways on how to attain good sleeping conditions.

  Doing it every now and then is not sufficient though. Good sleeping habits must be developed and sustained so as to better manage your weight.

- Removing yourself from extremely stressful situations

One of the many effects of stress hormones on the body is suppression of the digestive system. If you have not eaten yet, then it would end up ruining your appetite. On the other hand, if you have already eaten, then it might cause digestive problems since it would prevent proper digestion.

Stress could contribute to weight gain too if one of your preferred coping mechanism is eating food and/or imbibing copious amounts of alcohol. Associating stressful situations with the temporary relief that food or alcohol could provide may lead to numerous consequences for your general wellbeing.

o Reduced Vulnerability Towards Serious Illnesses and Infections

Since hygge promotes the practice of relaxing the body and the mind, getting enough quality sleep, and eating good food in the company of those you care about, it ultimately shields you from various types of diseases and illnesses that plague the modern man, such as:

- Different forms of cancer
- Cardiovascular diseases
- Neurodegenerative diseases
- Type 1 and Type 2 Diabetes
- Kidney-related problems

Do not think that hygge would cure you of these health problems though. It would help you prevent the onset of these diseases and illnesses because studies show that stress, poor diet, and lack of exercise and sleep could lead to disastrous consequences on one's health.

Hygge places great value on these things in life, so applying its principles to all aspects of life could significantly lower your chances of developing serious health problems now and later on.

- For the Mind

Studies show that creating and maintaining a hygge environment can help you achieve peace of mind and emotional stability. You would lessen your suffering from anxiety. You would be shielded from the constant bombardment caused by your fears and insecurities.

By protecting your mind through the practice of hygge, you would be able to experience the following mental benefits:

o   Less Likelihood of Depression

Hygge fights off the onset of depression, especially the kind that originates from the cold, dreary winters—seasonal affective disorder. Much like other forms of depression, SAD makes the person afflicted with it feel drops in their mood and energy levels. It could also exacerbate existing depression tendencies, thus severely impacting one's day to day activities.

While hygge is not capable of eliminating one's depression, it is highly effective in reducing a person's vulnerability towards this mood disorder. By encouraging people to seek comfort, warmth, and other people, hygge could minimize the effects of the harsh realities of life on your life.

There is no shortage on how you could begin adopting hygge principles as your way of life. In fact, the only rule seems to be is to go after what would make you feel happy and cozy. Several people comply with this by performing these hyggelig activities:

- Lighting up scented candles
- Cooking and savoring your favorite dish
- Spending the evening by the fireplace with your loved ones
- Taking a long, hot shower in the morning
- Dressing yourself up with the most comfortable pieces of clothing that you can find
- Reading a book while drinking a cup of hot chocolate
- Admiring the scenery as you breathe in and out in deliberate manner
- Putting down your cellphone and personally socializing with other people instead.
- Watching your favorite movie while cozying up under a woolen duvet

While many people find these measures effective in reducing their chances of developing depression, it does not mean that it would work for you as well. However, there is no significant harm in trying out something that could potentially relieve you from suffering. Just remember to seek out professional help when you notice that living the hygge way is not enough to combat your depressive tendencies.

o Prevents Excessive Bouts of Anxiety

Anxiety can be particularly intrusive to one's day to day life. It affects one's happiness, wellness, work performance, and relationships with other people. Anxiety, by itself, is a natural response of the body and mind towards danger and risks, However, it becomes a mental disorder when the worry and fear that you feel becomes too much and too persistent for you to handle.

In order to tell if the level of anxiety that you are feeling is troubling for your mental health, here are the common signs and symptoms of anxiety disorder:

- Feeling tensed, restless, or nervous frequently, or for extended periods of time
- Breathing in and out in a rapid pace
- Excessive sweating in different parts of the body, such as the forehead, neck, back, armpits, or palms of the hand
- Excessive trembling of the body
- Problems with appetite and digestion

- Believing that there is a danger or disaster that is waiting to happen, even when there is no proof to be had
- Trouble in focusing on the current task due to worries, doubts, or fears about other matters
- Inability to fall asleep or remain sleeping for the whole night
- Deliberately avoiding seeing or doing things that you may think will cause you to feel anxious

Though treatments and prescriptions may be given by mental health professionals to those who suffer from it, studies show that supplementing medication with therapy and the support from the people around you yields better results in the long term.

Hygge promotes togetherness, not only for entertainment purposes but also for seeking the support of others during times of need. When you feel burdened with your worries, doubts, and insecurities, turning to a person you trust for help and understanding can keep from devolving into an even worse state. Showing others that you show them your vulnerable side inspires trust, which ultimate results to stronger bonds with them.

Knowing that you have someone to back you up can do wonders for your mental and emotional stability. Build close relationships with the people around you by continually practicing hygge in every aspect of your life.

o   Increased Self-Compassion

If you think about it, hygge wants you to be kind to yourself, even it encourages you to spend quality time with the people you care about. That rings true, especially when you consider the belief that it is hard—if not impossible—to take care of others and your surroundings when you do not care about your wellbeing, too.

Based on this, you can say that you will start feeling the effects of hygge starts from within. The deliberate things you do to become happier, cozier, and more secure would eventually turn into something you do naturally for yourself.

Turning kindness inwards before extending it to others is a mark of a truly hyggelig lifestyle. Rather than stressing yourself out to the point of breakdown, you are able to appreciate the value of taking a well-deserved break whenever you need one.

o Greater Sense of Mindfulness

To be mindful is to have total awareness of your thoughts, feelings, or experience as they occur. Given such a definition, it is easy to see how the practice of hygge promotes mindfulness among its followers.

By focusing on the present, you would be able to appreciate the things that are happening to you, while reducing the ill effects of bad memories and worries about the future on your body and mind. Many people equate this with meditation, but a fine line exists between the two. Meditation does not require you to stay in the present, but mindfulness does. In this regard, hygge appears to be more connected with mindfulness than meditation per se.

o Provides More Opportunities to Practice Gratitude

In the midst of everything that must be done within the day, it can be easy to forget to be thankful of the small and big things that make you feel happy, cozy, and safe. Many people also take for granted the things people do for them, whether deliberately or unintentionally.

Practicing gratitude whenever and wherever you are is not only hyggelig. Studies show that a grateful mindset makes people healthier, too. It stabilizes one's emotions, and minimizes the effects of stressors on the body. They also benefit by getting stronger immune systems, and healthier cardiovascular systems.

Hygge living provides plenty of opportunities for one to practice gratitude. It encourages people to appreciate the time they spend with other people, and with nature. As such, it becomes easier to recognize the things that make them feel joy and comfort.

Being open to the positive aspects of life also gives way to a more expressive way of living. Rather than simply keeping your thoughts and emotions inside, those who follow the principles of hygge understand the value of sharing themselves with those they care about.

Furthermore, adopting gratitude as one of your core values encourages others to do so. This positive attitude tends to inspire other people to follow the same path. As a result, your social circles would become more supportive, generous, and optimistic.

Ultimately, freeing your mind from its burdens would help you open up more to the people around you. You feel secured about yourself, so letting others in would no longer incite apprehension or feelings of dread.

- For the Spirit

Though hygge is associated with specific physical objects, such as candles, knitted clothes, and hot beverages, its core principles are centered upon immaterial concepts. Rather than striving to own the said items, hygge is more about the feeling that they inspire within one's self. For example, candles can come in various colors and scents, but they would not be considered as hyggelig for you if you do not feel pleasant, relaxed, or happy whenever you light one up in your home.

Given this, you may say that hygge is actually a pratice that touches upon the body, mind, and soul. Its positive effects goes beyond improving one's physical health, and balancing one's emotions. It also enriches the spirit in ways that other types of lifestyle simply do not enable. For example:

o   Enhances your sense of belongingness to your family, friends, and community

One of the core principles of hygge is to establish and maintain strong connections with your family, friends, co-workers, and other people that you interact with. This may be achieved through various means, as long as the goal is to foster the ideas of togetherness, equality, harmony, and peace.

By prioritizing these values, you would be abe to keep yourself from seeking approval from other people. Instead, you could better focus on communicating with them in a manner that would inspire spiritual growth within you and the people around you.

o   Guides the path towards contentment

The practice of hygge places great emphasis on learning how to be contented with what you have instead desiring for unnecessary things in life. It preaches that money is not that important as long as you can afford the basic necessities that you need every day. In fact, too much of it could be disruptive in one's attempts to create genuine hyggelig moments.

Hygge is not about fine dining or splurging on a few luxury items for yourself. It is about handmade gifts and homecooked meals. Above all, it is finding joy in the simple things that are made with love and care.

Hygge also encourages people to look for the positive side of things, even when it seems like things are not exactly going your way. For example, your dishwasher has broken down while in the middle of washing your dishes. Rather than fuming about this sudden interruption, you could resolve to wash the dishes by hand instead while you listen to your favorite music as it plays in the background.

Discontentment breeds more negative feelings, such as deep resentment, anger, jealousy, and envy. Therefore, giving in to these urges must be avoided whenever possible. Hygge has proven to be excellent at planting and growing the seeds of contentment into one's spirit.

o Teaches a selfless manner to perform self-care measures

Some people might thing that selflessness and self-care has nothing to do with one another.

However, hyggelig living shows everyone that caring for one's self does not mean that you cannot take good care of other people.

Such core principle makes hygge quite special, especially for those seeking for refuge in these confusing and trying times. Some people who are not aware of the merits of self-care for the body, mind, and soul tend to forego its practice, thus missing out on numerous opportunities for growth and development. Those who understand, on the other hand, recognizes the value of making one's happiness and comfort a priority in order to bring about waves of positivity towards other people.

Many people think that by depriving themselves of food, water, or sleep, they would be performing a divine sacrifice for the good of everyone. However, what do these self-limiting practices actually do for the betterment of everyone involved? If you think about it in altruistic terms, not as much as what you can achieve when you take good care of yourself.

The thing is, you cannot start caring for other people when you do not know how to take care of yourself. Selfnessness, much like selfishness, begins within, but ends up moving in completely different paths. Hygge could guide you to the direction that could not only make you feel good, but also make others feel the same way.

As explained earlier, hygge has profound effects on your chances of making a strong and lasting connection with other people. Reaching out to others becomes a lot easier when you feel happy and secured with yourself.

Furthermore, the core guiding principles of hygge place great importance on establishing and maintaining good relationships with your family, friends, co-workers, and even with the people you have just met.

To better explain the positive effects of hygge on your relationships with other people, here is quick rundown of its numerous social benefits that you may expect:

- Improves the way you communicate with other people

  Having an open dialogue with others does not come naturally for everyone. In fact, most people struggle with communicating their thoughts and feelings in a healthy manner.

  Mastering the art of communication, however, would be quite an important achievement for anyone. With this, you may be able to experience significant personal growth, gain a deeper understanding of the world around you, and improve upon your relationships with other people—may it be a member of your family, a friend, a romantic partner, a co-worker, or someone that you have just met.

The Danish people have long recognized this importance, hence the emphasis on social wellness of hygge. For them, joy and comfort goes hand in hand with the familiarity gained through open communication.

By applying the principles of hygge on the way you hold conversations with others, you would be able to foster harmony, and encourage the sharing of wisdom and experiences between you and the people you care about.

For example, people nowadays feel like they have better things to do than chat with their co-workers during lunch break. Having this kind of mindset prevents them from engaging with others, and building closer ties in the long run. Rather than rush through the discussion just so you could get back to your desk, why not try taking your time to listen to what others have to say, and then say something thoughtful in return? You might end up discovering and learning new things that you are not expecting.

- Aids in developing stronger and deeper connections with the people you care about

Many people argue that the new ways of communication brought about recent technology has brought people closer, even when thousands of miles exist in between you and them. That may be true in terms of convenience, but it is not considered as a hygge

You might think that relationships gained and maintained through digital means and those fostered through hyggelig practices bears the same weight and significance for everyone. However, as demonstrated by the Danish people, their brand of social connection leads to more resilient, more supportive, and more fulfilling relationships in the long run.

Hygge is all about taking your sweet time when it comes to doing things for yourself, and that includes spending time with the people you cherish. It encourages you to invite people over, or to head over to someone else's place, just so you could share with them a personal conversation over cups of steaming hot tea. Hygge wants you to express how much you care about others through sincere words and acts of love, both of which are prone to losing some of their authenticity and meaning when delivered from a distance.

There are certain circumstances in life, however, when you cannot complete forego calling or texting someone from afar in order to stay connected with them. In such cases, hygge still wants you to focus on the quality rather than quantity.

Connect with them via video-calls rather than simply looking through their social media updates. Listen to their voice instead of simply messaging each other. Though such acts are not as hyggelig as spending time with them in person, doing these would be a lot better than not doing anything at all.

- Encourages and builds trust

As explained earlier, one of the core principles of hygge is authenticity. When considered along with its lessons about togetherness, you would realize that hygge promotes the formation of relationships that are built upon mutual trust.

You cannot expect others to trust you when you are not being honest about your thoughts, feelings, and actions. As such, in order to gain the trust of the people around you, you must learn how to be comfortable in staying true to yourself.

Hygge inspires you to grow that kind of confidence over time. By opening up to others and listening to what they have to say, you would eventually feel a sense of belongingness with them. Over time, you would learn to trust them more and more that even when faced with challenges, you know that you can count on them no matter what.

- Less dependence on social media

To practice hygge, you must learn how to step away from the digital world, and start living once more in the here and now. Put your cellphone down, and have a face-to-face conversation instead with those around you. Doing so would help you build deeper and more organic relationships that have solid foundations.

Studies also show that frequently browsing one's social media feed could exponentially increase the chances of developing depression and anxiety. Forgetting that social media accounts tend to reflect only the sides of people that they are comfortable sharing with others could make one feel discontentment and worry about his/her own quality of life and personal experiences.

Jealousy and envy, as well as overall dissatisfaction about one's life, could deteriorate the relationships that you have with yourself and with those you care about.

Instead of imagining a good and exciting life for yourself, hygge wants you to try and live it now. It does not limit anyone to a standard way of living, but rather this lifestyle is about going after what would make you feel happy, cozy, and secure.

If staying indoors and reading a book is what makes you happy, then you do not have to force yourself to go out on trips every weekend just because your friend from college keeps doing so. Conversely, if you enjoy a more rustic way of living, then you do not have to keep up with the trends just because everyone else keeps posting about it. Stay true to yourself, and enjoy life as you see fit. Others would surely appreciate your honesty and authenticity.

Hygge focuses on feeling comfortable and relaxed while connecting with other people and the environment. Learning how to practice it on a sustainable level would enable you to reap numerous benefits for your body, mind, soul, and relationships. Given these, everything that you may have to do in order to apply hygge across different aspects of your life is going to be worth your time and effort.

Chapter 3

Lighting Up Your
Home the Hygge Way

Experts in hygge know that combining the lamps and various candles results to an even more inviting and cozy atmosphere. However, setting up ambient lighting is not enough to capture the essence of a truly hyggelig home.

Creating a warm glow involves the application of hygge on different aspects of the house. As such, there are a lot of ways on how you could go about this. Here are the best ones that you should consider doing for your house:

- Hyggekrog

  Many followers of hygge believe that one of the essential things a home must have is a hyggekrog, a Danish term that loosely translates to "nook". Basically, a hyggekrog is any space within the home that may be used as the primary location for simple hyggelig activities, such as reading a book, drinking hot chocolate, or curling up under a woolen blanket.

This special place does not have to be fancy, nor does it have to be constructed specifically for this purpose. Just look around your home, and observe which spot would be best for relaxing and warming yourself up. For example, a lot of people opt to place an armchair by a window that offers a nice view of the outdoors. There, they could sit comfortably while performing various hyggelig activities, such as knitting and meditation. This choice is particularly popular in Denmark, where it is common to see bay windows that are furnished with fluffy cushions and blankets.

To guide you in choosing the ideal place to set up a hyggekrog in your home, here is a set of criteria that you may refer to. Keep in mind that you do not have to conform with whatever the other people are doing. Take heed of what you want for yourself in order to better apply the hygge principles in your home.

- You believe staying in this place would make your body and mind feel relaxed.
- It has ample but soft lighting.
- The space is big enough for you and at least one other person.
- Furnishing it the hygge way would not cause you too much money.
- Fireplace

According to a recent survey conducted among Danish households, three out of ten homes in Denmark feature either a fireplace or a stove that uses wood as its primary fuel. In comparison, only one in 28 homes in the UK have installed such amenities. Given these numbers, it is easy to see that the hygge-loving people of Denmark recognizes the special properties of a simple fireplace.

In the US alone, more than half of the recently constructed homes have a fireplace. Compared to nearly forty years ago, only a third of the households have this feature. Furthermore, the survey revealed that it is considered by many potential house buyers as one of the most sought-after amenities in a residential property.

But what exactly makes a fireplace so popular? According to another survey conducted among the Danes, they have two main reasons for their preference on having a fireplace in their home. Of the two reasons, the lesser one pertains to the fact that a fireplace is a relatively cheap source of warmth, especially during winter where the heating must be kept on at all times. The primary reason, however, lies on the close association with hygge. Almost 70 percent of the respondents agreed that installing a fireplace somewhere in the house turns it into a warm, relaxing, and joy-filled home.

Having learned the core principles of hygge, it is easy to see why those people believe in such notions. The fireplace is somewhere you could comfortably stay at while sipping tea under cozy blankets with your loved ones.

- Candles

Candles play a huge role in a hygge-based lifestyle. In fact, most people, particularly Danes, say that this object best represents the concept itself. The Danish term for "spoilsport"—lyseslukker—literally translates to "the person who puts out the candle". They also light candles in places that are not commonly chosen by other cultures, such as classrooms, offices, and retail shops. Foreigners might think of them as merely fire hazards, but for Danes, they are excellent sources for comfort and happiness.

This level of association between the two likely stems from the belief that the fastest way to adopt hygge is by lighting a few candles inside your home. That instantly creates a warm, pleasant atmosphere—the kind that invites people to stay, chat, and relax together.

However, studies show that this heightened desire for candles result to a potentially harmful consequence—the release of additional soot in the air. The Danish have taken upon themselves to study this phenomenon. Through this, they were able to learn that candles release more micro-particles when lighten indoors compared to cigarettes. These particles may cause serious health problems, particularly to the lungs.

Interestingly, this observation did not significantly lessen the market for candles among the Danes. They just conducted further studies to determine appropriate measures that would protect them from the negative effects of soot on their health.

If you are not as obsessed with candles as the Danes, there are several other hyggelig lighting options that you can consider using in order to create the right kind of atmosphere.

- Wooden Things

The Danes have an ongoing love affair with anything made of wood. Various studies point out that since wood is simple and natural, it helps the Danish people feel a deeper connection with nature—which is also one of the foundational principles of hygge.

There are various ways to incorporate more wood into your home. For many, the easiest way is to get some beautiful wooden furniture, such as benches, tables, chairs, or bed frames.

Others make it a point to use wooden materials during the construction of the home itself. This means wooden flooring or walls—oftentimes, both.

The smell of wood also inspires hyggelig feelings. That is why many Danes enjoy spending time in front of a crackling fireplace, where the aroma from the burning wood could make anyone feel relaxed and at home.

Recently, there is a growing trend in Denmark for wooden toys for children rather than plastic ones. This means that the love for wooden things may be instilled to the next generation at an even younger age.

You might have concerns regarding the effect of wooden furniture and decorations for the environment. To lessen your worries, choose pieces that have already been used by others, and just restore them to their former glories instead.

- Nature-Inspired Decorations

Getting wooden furniture and home décor is simply not enough for the Danish people. To truly showcase their commitment to hygge, they try to bring as much of the forest as they can inside their homes. This means that anything that could enable you to feature a piece of nature in your home is likely going to be considered as hyggelig. For example:

- o   Dried leaves and flowers
- o   Twigs with interesting textures or forms
- o   Animal skins, e.g. cowhide, sheepskin, reindeer fur

Based on this list, what you can do is embellish your wooden furniture and plush couches with animal skin. Lay a cowhide rug on the floor for an extra boost of hygge. Then, hang around the room some framed leaves and flowers, as well as preserved twigs.

Since you would most likely light up some candles to complete the look you are going for, make sure to take precautionary measures to avoid accidentally setting things on fire. These nature-inspired decorations are highly flammable after all.

- •   Books

Spending your free time by reading a book while sitting on a plush armchair is extremely hyggelig. As such, it is highly recommended to furnish your home with shelves that are filled with your favorite books.

Hygge does not impose limits on the genre of books that you should read. May it be romance, adventure, sci-fi, horror, or even cookbooks, as long as reading a book stirs hyggelig feelings within you, you are free to include that in your book collection.

For an extra dose of hygge, create a readers' club among your family and friends so that you can spend time with them while enjoying this hobby that is usually done alone. You may also want to invite your kids, or the kids of your family members or friends for a book reading session. In this way, you would be able to instill within them the value of a good book.

- Different Kinds of Texture

Applying the hyggelig principles to your home is not just about creating a certain look. It is also about experiencing the right kind of feel. Combining textures, such as wood, fur, metal, and ceramic, adds a dynamic layer to your home, which then inspire you to feel more joy, relaxation, warmth, and comfort.

To do this, think about the distinct feeling that you want to incorporate into your personal space. Do you feel more comfortable by being surrounded by furry throws, and minimalistic but plush cushions? Or are you someone who prefers touching wood rather than steel or glass?

Make things interesting by diversifying the kinds of texture that may be found in your home. There is no right or combination though. Remember, the key is finding something that makes you feel happy, cozy, warm, and safe.

- Vintage Items

The Danish people places a great value on things that are considered as vintage. Antique shops may be found all over Denmark, offering a wide array of unique finds from different generations and periods. This does not mean, however, that anything old would do. In hygge, the goal when shopping for vintage items is to find the diamond among the coals.

If you are used to assessing the value of antique finds, then here are a couple of tips that you would surely find handy:

o Read or ask about the history of the item.

Some antique shops make it a point to place cards or signage indicating where the item has originated, what it has gone through over the years, how the shop has managed to find it, and other similar pieces of information that makes the item even more interesting.

If such information could not be found anywhere in the shop, then you may reach out to the staff or owner of the antique shop. Ask them about the given points. More often than not, they would be glad to share with you what they know because those who shop for antiques usually look for something with a storied past, or at least a fascinating origin.

○ Reflect upon your past, and see if the item connects with something you treasure from before.

By doing so, you would be able to have an initial emotional value for the item you are looking at. Nostalgic feelings is considered by many as hyggelig because it normally makes one long for the good times spent with family and friends.

To do this, think about a point in your past where a similar item has appeared. It may be an armchair that closely resembles the one your grandma sat on while knitting Christmas sweaters. Perhaps, it is wardrobe that looks like the one you used as the perfect hiding spot when playing hide-and-seek with your siblings and cousins.

Recall those memories and how you felt at the time. Observe if the item could potentially inspire similar feelings within you. In this way, you would make a purchase that is not only aesthetically pleasing, but is also emotionally valuable.

o Evaluate the item in terms of how hyggelig it is for you.

Look at the item you wish to buy. Touch it, and smell it—if applicable. Get a better sense of what feelings the item is stirring within you.

Once you have done so, ask yourself these questions:

- Does it make you feel joy and comfort?
- Would it inspire feelings of warmth for you and your loved ones?
- How would the item affect the overall feel of the place where you wish to put it in?

It is important to consider the value for money of the item as well. Hygge promotes the idea of frugal living, so spending a lot of money on something could only be warranted if the said item would bring a lot of value for you. Check if it is also within your current means. Refrain from spending more than you can afford. Otherwise, purchasing the item might not be hyggelig for you after all.

- Blankets and Cushions

A hyggelig home would not be complete without cozy blankets and fluffy pillows. These items are the easiest ways to boost the comfort factor of any space, especially during the cold season.

Even when it is not winter, snuggling under a blanket, especially with a loved one, is extremely hyggelig. For those who live in colder climates, the best kind of material is either wool or rabbit fur. On the other hand, those who reside in tropic regions would likely appreciate blankets made of cotton.

In terms of cushions, you may go for whichever size you want to have in your home. You can vary your selection as well, so that you can have cushions that may be used for additional seating when you have guests over, and small ones that you can use to make yourself feel more comfortable when you lounge on the couch.

Reflecting the Warmth of Your Home on Your Clothes

Hygge goes beyond creating ambience within your home, or spending quality time with your family and friends. It also encourages the practice of self-care whenever possible.

Clothing is a basic necessity for humans. What you choose to wear every day affects your mood, your behavior, and the way others would treat you. Therefore, it is important to combine the principles of hygge and fashion in order to feel good about yourself while looking stylish in the same process.

To dress yourself up like a Danish, follow these guidelines for hyggelig clothing:

- Black clothing reigns supreme.

  Fashion-wise, hygge encourages its followers to wear something in black instead of any other color. If this dark color is not for you, then at least choose something that has a subdued tone, like dark gray, brown, or midnight blue.

  Avoid pairing up contrasting or complementing colors as well—at least in your clothing. Go for a monochromatic look, and play things up using various clothing textures and patterns instead.

- Wear thick scarves

  The concept of hygge has elevated the status of this simple accessory as a must-have for both men and women. Though it is primarily worn during winter, many people may be observed wearing one at the first sign of fall.

In hygge, the bigger the scarf, the better it is. Therefore, silk scarves may be quite pleasant to touch, but for a more hyggelig experience, go for knitted or woolen variants that could go at least twice around your neck.

- Opt for comfortable tops.

For your reference, here are the most popular types of hyggelig tops that you should start incorporating into your wardrobe:

  o Cardigans
  o Jumpers
  o Pull-overs
  o Sweaters

To add in an extra dose of hygge, choose tops that are knitted by hand using materials, such as wool or cotton. Since the given types of tops tend to be bulky and heavy, you can even things out by wearing dark-colored slim-cut jeans or leggings.

If you want to truly emulate Danish fashion, then you should in arguably the most popular type of sweater among the Danes—the Sarah Lund sweater.

Its wide appeal among hygge enthusiasts started when the design was featured in the hit Danish TV show "The Killing", wherein one of its characters, Sarah Lund, first donned the now-iconic sweater. According to Sofie Grabol, the actress who played the said character, the homely design of the sweater shows how at peace Sarah Lund is with herself. The character does not have to wear a suit to reflect how high her self-confidence is.

Furthermore, Sofie explained that the sweater reminded her of the clothing that her hippie parents wore back in the seventies. As such, the Sarah Lund sweater also promotes the values of companionship and coziness.

- Layer your clothes.

  This applies particularly to those who live in colder regions, or to those who live in places where the weather tends to be quite unpredictable.

  Donning layered clothing, such as coats or jackets over a pair of sweater vest and button-downs, on a chilly day would make you feel warmer and more comfortable compared when you just wear only a thick sweater.

  In case the temperature rises some time during the day, you may easily shed off the additional layers without the hassle of going back home just to change your clothes.

  If you are leaving the house while the sun is out, it is best to bring with you a cardigan. By doing so, you can switch into more comfortable clothes when the temperature drops by evening. Hygge is impossible to achieve when you feel cold after all.

- Indulge yourself with comfortable woolen socks.

  They may not be the most fashionable piece of clothing that you can get for yourself, but woolen socks are supremely hyggelig. Get a set that bears your favorite colors and patterns. In this way, you can easily slip on a pair whenever you feel the need to snuggle up in your couch alone or with a loved one.

  If socks are not your thing, then you may indulge your fee with a pair of fur-lined slippers. This type of indoor footwear comes with high recommendations from the hygge experts—just make sure to get ones that are made of faux fur rather than animal fur. Faux fur is a lot friendlier to both your wallet and the environment.

If you do not have these items yet in your current wardrobe, then you would have to go out and purchase some pieces for yourself. This may seem like something that would go against the core principle of hygge for minimal and frugal living, but only if you do not make it a point to purchasing clothing in a thoughtful manner.

Rather than buying something because it is on sale, or because you just want to get this over with, you should take the time to evaluate what you really need and want to wear.

Discounts are only hyggelig when you get them while purchasing an item that truly inspires joy and excitement within you, even without the discount in the first place.

Another effective way of making thoughtful purchases is by making an item a reward for a personal accomplishment. For example, you have decided to keep yourself fit by going out for a jog around the park every morning. As a way of reinforcing this healthy habit, you should reward yourself with something you really want to have when you manage to do your morning jogging for 30 days without fail.

Doing this would remind of your great accomplishment whenever you see or use that special item. Moreover, it would keep you from making unnecessary purchases while you are working towards your goal.

Chapter 4

Delighting Your Taste Buds with Hyggelig Food and Beverages

Following a hyggelig lifestyle is not possible without learning some key dishes that could bring about joy, comfort, and togetherness for everyone at the dinner table. It is not the food itself though, nor the hot drinks served in dainty cups.

Hyggelig food is all about the aroma of spices blended together into one savory dish. It is the curl of hot steam emanating from your favorite tea. It is the sound of the gentle stirring as you prepare your breakfast oats.

These recipes are made extra special, not because of the ingredients used or the techniques applied. The following recipes are considered hyggelig due to the care and attention that goes into their preparation, and the kind of feelings that they could inspire out of those who would get to enjoy these meals.

Learn how to relax your body, calm your mind, and soothe your soul through the hyggelig recipes given below. The dishes are divided according to the perfect meal of the day where each one may be served. However, feel free to mix and match based on which one would make you feel the happiest. As a bonus, an extra section for traditional desserts and welcoming drinks can be found at the latter part of this chapter.

Enjoy!

Breakfast

- Energizing Nutty Oats with Pumpkin Seeds

  Get an energy boost from this savory-sweet breakfast delight.

  o Ingredients:

    - 1 cup steel-cut oats
    - 8 figs, sliced
    - 1 cup walnuts, chopped
    - ½ cup coconut flakes, unsweetened
    - 1/3 cup pumpkin seeds
    - 2 tablespoons birch tree syrup
    - 1 teaspoon sea salt
    - 1 teaspoon pumpkin seed oil

  o Approximate Prep Time: 40 minutes

  o Yield: Makes 4 servings

- Directions:

  1. Boil the oats with salt and 4 cups of water in a large pot.
  2. Lower the heat to medium.
  3. Cook without the lid on for 25 minutes.
  4. Toast the walnuts, coconut flakes, and pumpkin seeds in a large skillet for 2 minutes, or until the coconut flakes begin turning light brown.
  5. Get enough toasted toppings for your oats, while storing the rest in an air-tight container.
  6. Divide equally the cooked oats into 4 bowls.
  7. Top with the toasted nuts, coconut, and seeds.
  8. Drizzle with birch tree syrup and pumpkin seed oil.
  9. Serve with buttermilk, if desired.

- Tropical Zest Yoghurt Loaf

Make your morning extra special with this sweet and savory treat.

- Ingredients:

  - 3 fresh eggs

- 1 2/3 cup all-purpose flour, sifted
- 1 cup brown sugar
- 1 cup crushed pineapples, drained
- 2/3 cup plain yoghurt
- ½ cup raisins
- 1/3 cup shredded coconut, sweetened
- ¼ cup orange zest
- 6 tablespoons unsalted butter, at ambient temperature
- 2 teaspoons baking powder
- ¼ teaspoon salt
- ¼ teaspoon ground cinnamon

- Approximate Prep & Baking Time: 75 minutes

- Yield: Makes 12 to 16 servings

- Directions:

  1. Preheat the oven to 325 ºF.
  2. Grease a 9-inch by 5-inch loaf pan.
  3. Combine well the butter and sugar in a bowl.
  4. Add one egg at a time into the bowl. Make sure that each egg has been blended well before adding the next one.
  5. Add the yoghurt and orange zest.

6. Using a separate bowl, combine the sifted flour, baking powder, cinnamon, and salt.

7. Pour the dry ingredients into the butter mixture.

8. Stir in the pineapples, raisins, and shredded coconut.

9. Pour the mixture into the greased loaf pan.

10. Bake for 60 minutes, or until the tester comes out clean when poked into the center of the bread.

11. Let the loaf bread cool down for 30 minutes.

12. Remove from the pan, and transfer into a cooling rack.

13. Cut into thick slices, and serve with hot coffee or tea.

- Smoked Trout on Toasted Bread

Start your day right with a light and refreshing open-faced sandwich.

  o Ingredients:

    ▪ 2 slices pumpernickel rye bread
    ▪ 1 pack smoked rainbow trout, thinly sliced
    ▪ 1 large egg, boiled, peeled and sliced
    ▪ 2 cherry tomatoes, thinly sliced

- 1 small cucumber, thinly sliced
- 1 radish, thinly sliced
- ½ cup mayonnaise
- 2 tablespoons fresh dill, finely chopped
- 2 tablespoons fresh chives, finely chopped
- 1 teaspoon lemon juice, freshly squeezed
- 1 teaspoon lemon rind, freshly grated

- Approximate Prep Time: 25 minutes

- Yield: Makes 4 servings

- Directions:

  1. Lightly toast both sides of the rye bread slices.
  2. Divide each slice into two.
  3. In a small bowl, combine mayonnaise, dill, chives, lemon juice, and lemon rind.
  4. Spread evenly on one side of each toast.
  5. Top each with sliced smoked trout.
  6. Garnish with various combinations of boiled egg, tomatoes, cucumber, and radish.
  7. Serve with lemon wedges, if desired.

Lunch

- Slow-Cooked Swedish Meatballs with Lingonberry Gravy

  Enjoy a filling and tasty meal that you can cook and serve using the same pot.

  - Ingredients:
    - 1 pound ground turkey
    - 1 pound ground pork
    - 2 large eggs
    - 1 cup beef broth
    - ½ cup breadcrumbs
    - ½ cup fresh parsley, chopped
    - ¼ cup sour cream
    - 3 tablespoons unsalted butter, at ambient temperature
    - 3 tablespoons all-purpose flour
    - 1 tablespoon Worcestershire sauce
    - 1 tablespoon lingonberry jelly
    - 1 ½ teaspoon ground all-spice
    - 1 teaspoon kosher salt
    - 1 teaspoon black pepper, freshly grinded
    - 1 teaspoon onion powder
  - Approximate Prep & Cooking Time: 160 minutes

- Yield: Makes 10 to 12 servings

- Directions:

  1. Pour the beef broth and Worcestershire in a medium-sized slow cooker.
  2. Combine ground turkey, ground pork, eggs, breadcrumbs, all-spice, salt, pepper, and onion powder in a large bowl.
  3. Gently mix together the ingredients until the color and texture appear uniform all throughout.
  4. Turn the mixture into balls using your hands, one spoonful at a time.
  5. Arrange the meatballs in a single layer inside the slow cooker.
  6. Once the bottom layer is filled with meatballs, add another layer on top of it.
  7. Cover the slow cooker with its lid.
  8. Cook on a high setting for 120 minutes, or until the meatballs have been cooked through.
  9. While waiting, create a smooth paste by mixing the butter and flour in a small bowl.
  10. Form 0.5-inch balls from the butter-flour balls. Set aside.

11. Remove the meatballs from the slow cooker using a slotted spoon, and transfer into a large bowl. Set aside.
12. Stir in the butter-flour balls—1 or 2 balls at a time—into the remaining meatball juices in the slow cooker.
13. Add the sour cream and lingonberry jelly into the mixture.
14. Stir well until the sauce looks even in color and texture.
15. Return the cooked meatballs to the slow cooker.
16. Coat each meatball with the lingonberry gravy.
17. Cook in the slow cooker without the lid on using the high setting for 30 minutes, or until the sauce has thickened.
18. Top with chopped parsley before serving.

- Cheesy French Onion Soup Casserole

Elevate your meal by preparing this classic French dish.

  o Ingredients:

    - 4 cups Spanish onion, thinly sliced
    - 6 1-inch slices French baguette, lightly toasted

- 2 ½ cups beef stock
- 1 cup gruyere cheese, shredded
- ½ cup parmesan, shredded
- 2 sprigs fresh thyme
- 3 tablespoons unsalted butter, at ambient temperature
- 2 tablespoons white wine, preferably Madeira wine
- 1 tablespoon salted butter, melted
- 1 tablespoon Worcestershire sauce
- 1 teaspoon salt
- 1 teaspoon black pepper, freshly ground

- Approximate Prep & Cooking Time: 90 minutes

- Yield: Makes 6 servings

- Directions:

  1. Melt the butter on a pan using the medium heat.
  2. Add the onion slices and salt into the pan.
  3. Caramelize the onions in butter by stirring intermittently until they have gained a deep brown color.
  4. Pour and stir in the white wine.

5. Continue cooking for about 1 minute, or until the alcohol has been absorbed by the onions
6. Preheat the oven to 400 °F.
7. Add the beef stock, thyme, Worcestershire sauce, salt, and pepper into the pan.
8. Cook for about 5 minutes, or until the stock has been reduced to a third.
9. Transfer the contents of the pan into casserole dish.
10. Arrange and press down the baguette slices on top of the onion mixture.
11. Wait until the baguette slices are completely soaked with the mixture.
12. Top the casserole with shredded cheese and melted butter.
13. Bake the mixture for about 30 minutes, or until the cheese has gained a golden brown color.
14. Serve immediately.

- Risotto with Butternut Squash and Saffron

Bring in the autumnal colors and flavors through this special dish.

- o Ingredients:

  - 2 ounces pancetta, diced
  - 6 cups butternut squash, peeled and cubed
  - 6 cups chicken stock
  - 6 tablespoons unsalted butter
  - 1 ½ cups rice
  - 1 cup parmesan cheese, freshly grated
  - ½ cup shallots, minced
  - ½ cup dry white wine
  - 2 tablespoons extra-virgin olive oil
  - 1 teaspoon saffron threads
  - 1 teaspoon kosher salt
  - 1 teaspoon black pepper, freshly ground

- o Approximate Prep & Cooking Time: 60 minutes

- o Yield: Makes 4 to 6 servings

- o Directions:

  1. Preheat the oven to 400 °F.
  2. Arrange the butternut squash cubes on a sheet pan.
  3. Drizzle and toss it with olive oil, salt, and pepper.
  4. Roast for 25 minutes, or until the squash has become tender. Remember to toss them again once midway.

5. While waiting, simmer the chicken stock in a saucepan with lid over low heat.

6. In a Dutch oven, melt the butter before adding the pancetta and shallows.

7. Sauté using medium-high heat for 10 minutes, or until the shallots have become translucent.

8. Stir in the rice grains until they have become coated with butter.

9. Pour the wine, and cook for another 2 minutes.

10. Add 2 cups of stock, saffron, salt, and pepper to the rice.

11. Stir before simmering for 10 minutes, or until the liquid has been mostly absorbed.

12. Remove from the heat.

13. Add the roasted butternut squash and cheese.

14. Stir well before serving.

Dinner

- Pork Tenderloin Roast with Savory Balsamic Rub

This traditional roasted pork dish can make any meal special and comforting. Why wait for the holidays to serve a feast for your family or guests?

- o Ingredients:
  - ▪ 4 ½ pounds pork tenderloin
  - ▪ 8 cloves garlic, cracked
  - ▪ 4 sprigs fresh thyme, de-stemmed and finely chopped
  - ▪ 4 sprigs fresh rosemary, de-stemmed and finely chopped
  - ▪ 4 tablespoons balsamic vinegar
  - ▪ 4 tablespoons extra-virgin olive oil
  - ▪ 1 tablespoon kosher salt
  - ▪ 1 tablespoon black pepper, freshly grinded
- o Approximate Prep & Cooking Time: 30 minutes
- o Yield: Makes 10 servings
- o Directions:
  1. Pre-heat the oven to 500 ºF.
  2. Remove the connective tissues from the tenderloin.
  3. Place the trimmed tenderloin on a non-stick rimmed baking sheet.
  4. Rub a few tablespoons of balsamic vinegar on the meat.
  5. Lightly coat the meat with olive oil.
  6. Create small slits on the meat.

7. Spread chunks of cracked garlic across different portions of the tenderloin.
8. Mix the salt, pepper, thyme and rosemary in a small bowl.
9. Rub the tenderloin with the dry mix.
10. Roast in the oven for 20 minutes.
11. Allow the roasted meat to rest before carving it.
12. Arrange the slices in a platter, and serve.

- Sweet and Sour Smoked Salmon

  Enjoy this zesty but savory dish with the whole family.

  o Ingredients:

    - 2 ½-pound salmon fillets
    - 2 large oranges, peeled and halved
    - 2 cups brown sugar
    - 1 cup maple syrup
    - 1 cup kosher salt
    - ¼ cup orange zest
    - 1 tablespoon black
    - 1 pepper, freshly ground
    - 1 teaspoon ground coriander seed
    - 1 teaspoon ground juniper berries

  o Approximate Prep & Cooking Time: 165 minutes

o Yield: Makes 6 servings

o Directions:

1. Mix the sugar, salt, orange zest, pepper, ground coriander seed, and ground juniper berries in a bowl.

2. Apply the mixture on all sides of the salmon fillets.

3. Arrange the crusted salmon fillets on a lined baking sheet with the skin-side down.

4. Store in the refrigerator for 90 minutes.

5. Remove the crust by running the salmon fillets under cold water.

6. Pat the salmon fillets dry using paper towel.

7. Cook the salmon fillets in a smoker grill for about 45 minutes, or until the salmon flakes when poked with a fork. Make sure to brush the salmon fillets with maple syrup every 5 minutes.

8. Broil the orange halves with the cut-side up.

9. Continue roasting until the oranges are charred.

10. Squeeze the charred oranges over the smoked salmon fillets before serving.

- Creamy Scalloped Potatoes

Who says hyggelig food is not for vegans? This exceptional take on potatoes would surely delight anyone's taste buds.

  o Ingredients:

    - 2 pounds yellow potatoes, sliced into 0.2-inch round cuts
    - 8 ounces silken tofu
    - 1 medium-sized onion, chopped
    - 1 clove garlic
    - 1 ½ cups almond milk, unsweetened and chilled
    - 1 cup almonds, lightly toasted
    - 1 cup water
    - ¼ cup fresh parsley, chopped
    - ¼ cup fresh thyme, de-stemmed
    - 3 tablespoons extra-virgin olive oil
    - 2 tablespoons almonds, blanched and sliced
    - 2 tablespoons lemon juice, freshly squeezed
    - 2 tablespoons nutritional yeast

- 1 teaspoon kosher salt
- 1 teaspoon black pepper, freshly ground

o Approximate Prep & Cooking Time: 105 minutes

o Yield: Makes 6 to 8 servings

o Directions:

1. Place a rack in the middle of the oven.
2. Preheat the oven to 375 °F.
3. Grease the sides and bottom of a baking dish.
4. In a food processor, combine the tofu, garlic, toasted almonds, yeast, lemon juice, salt, and pepper.
5. Pulse until the mixture becomes smooth.
6. Heat the oil in a skillet using the medium-high setting of the stove.
7. Add the onions.
8. Stir and cook for about 6 minutes, or until the onions have turned golden brown and soft.
9. Remove the skillet from the heat.
10. Stir in the parsley and thyme.
11. Pour the mixture into a bowl, and set aside.

12. Place the skillet back on the stove with medium heat.
13. Add the potatoes, almond milk, salt, and water.
14. Gently toss the potatoes with the use of a rubber spatula for 15 minutes, or until the liquid has thickened and the potatoes have become tender.
15. Scoop out the half of the potatoes into the baking dish, and arrange them evenly in a single layer.
16. Season the layer with salt and pepper.
17. Pour half of the processed tofu mixture and a third of the onion-herb mixture into the first layer.
18. Add the remaining potatoes as a second layer and repeat steps 16 and 17.
19. Cover the baking dish with foil.
20. Bake for 30 minutes.
21. Remove the cover before baking for another 15 minutes, or until the top has become bubbly and golden brown.
22. Take out of the oven to cool down before serving.

Desserts & Warming Drinks

- Baked Rice Pudding

  You do not have to slave away at the kitchen for the whole day just to enjoy this traditional Danish dessert. Here's how.

  - Ingredients:

    - 2 cups milk
    - 1 cup light cream
    - ½ cup long-grain white rice
    - ¼ cup white sugar
    - 2 tablespoons salted butter, at ambient temperature
    - 1 teaspoon orange zest
    - 1 teaspoon vanilla extract
    - ½ teaspoon ground cinnamon

  - Approximate Prep & Baking Time: 95 minutes

  - Yield: Makes 4 to 6 servings

  - Directions:

    1. Preheat the oven to 350 °F.
    2. Rinse well the rice grains.
    3. Drain the excess water, and then set aside.

4. Combine the milk, light cream, orange zest, vanilla extract, and cinnamon in a saucepan.
5. Boil the mixture.
6. Remove from the heat.
7. Stir in immediately the sugar and butter.
8. Let it cool for 15 minutes.
9. Stir in the rice grains into the mixture.
10. Transfer the contents of the saucepan into a baking dish.
11. Cover the dish with foil.
12. Bake for 75 minutes, stirring it halfway.
13. Serve while it is warm.

- Hyggelig Cinnamon Rolls

Curl up under the blanket while savoring this dessert and a cup of your favorite hot beverage.

  o Ingredients:

    - 1 pound frozen dough, thawed
    - ¾ cup powdered sugar
    - 1/3 cup hazelnuts, lightly toasted and chopped
    - ¼ cup dark brown sugar, packed
    - 3 tablespoons salted butter, melted
    - 3 tablespoons mascarpone cheese

- 2 tablespoons white sugar
- 1 tablespoon buttermilk
- 1 teaspoon ground cinnamon
- 1/8 teaspoon ground cloves

o Approximate Prep & Baking Time: 75 minutes

o Yield: Makes 6 servings

o Directions:

1. Brush melted butter on the bottom and side of a baking dish.
2. Combine the hazelnuts, brown sugar, white sugar, cinnamon, and cloves in a bowl.
3. Spread the dough on a 12-inch by 9-inch surface that has a light sprinkling of flour.
4. Brush melted butter on top of the dough.
5. Pour the hazelnut mixture on the dough, leaving a half-inch border on the top and bottom edges.
6. Roll up the dough starting on long side to form a log.
7. Pinch the seams to seal the log.
8. Cut the log into 9 even slices.
9. Arrange the sliced rolls with the cut side up on the baking dish. Make sure to leave at least a 1-inch space in between each roll.

10. Cover the dish with plastic wrap.
11. Leave the covered dish in ambient temperature for about 45 minutes, or until the rolls have risen up to your preferred size.
12. Preheat the oven to 325 °F.
13. Bake the rolls without a cover for 25 minutes, or until they have become golden brown.
14. While waiting, combine the powdered sugar, mascarpone cheese, and buttermilk in a separate bowl.
15. Stir until the mixture has become creamy and smooth.
16. Brush the remaining melted butter on top of the rolls.
17. Drizzle the creamy cheese mixture over the cinnamon rolls.
18. Serve while still warm.

- Caramel Apple Delight

This traditional Scandinavian dish could make you feel nostalgic for the good ol' days.

   o Ingredients:

      ▪ 3 medium-sized apples, peeled, cored and chopped
      ▪ 3 large eggs

- ¾ cup whole milk
- ¾ cup whole-wheat pastry flour
- 3 tablespoons unsalted butter
- 3 tablespoons white sugar
- 1 teaspoon vanilla extract
- 1 teaspoon kosher salt
- ½ teaspoon ground cinnamon
- ¼ teaspoon lemon zest, freshly grated
- confectioner's sugar (optional)

- Approximate Prep & Baking Time: 90 minutes

- Yield: Makes 4 servings

- Directions:

  1. Preheat the oven to 400 ºF.
  2. Combine the eggs and milk using a high-powered a blender.
  3. Add the flour, vanilla extract, salt, cinnamon, and lemon zest into the blender.
  4. Pulse for 15 seconds.
  5. Pour the contents into a bowl before chilling the mixture in the refrigerator.
  6. Melt the butter in an oven-safe pan using medium heat.
  7. Add the chopped apples and sugar.

8. Reduce the heat to low.

9. Cook while stirring intermittently for 20 minutes, or until the apples have become soft and golden brown.

10. Remove the pan from the heat.

11. Stir the chilled batter mix before pouring it over the cooked apples.

12. Bake for 30 minutes, or until the batter has risen for about 1.5 inches and has turned golden brown in color.

13. Dust with confectioner's sugar, if desired.

14. Serve directly using the pan, or transfer into your favorite serving plate.

- Mulled Cider

Fill your home with the soothing aroma of allspice, cinnamon, and cloves by preparing this drink.

  o Ingredients:

    ▪ 8 cups apple cider
    ▪ 2 allspice berries
    ▪ 2 sticks cinnamon
    ▪ 2 whole cloves
    ▪ 1 large orange, thinly sliced

- o Approximate Prep & Cooking Time: 15 minutes

- o Yield: Makes 8 servings

- o Directions:

  1. Combine all the ingredients in a large saucepan.
  2. Bring to a simmer using low heat.
  3. Pour into your favorite mugs.
  4. Serve while the drinks are hot.

- Mulled Wine

Turn a bottle of wine into a hyggelig experience by following this recipe.

- o Ingredients:

  - 1 bottle red wine
  - 4 whole cloves
  - 3 pieces star anise
  - 2 cinnamon sticks
  - 4 cups apple cider
  - ¼ cup raw honey
  - 1 medium-sized orange, juiced and zested

- o Approximate Prep & Cooking Time: 20 minutes

- o Yield: Makes 8 servings

o   Directions:

1. Mix together in a large saucepan the wine, cloves, star anise, cinnamon sticks, apple cider, honey, orange juice, and orange zest.
2. Bring the contents of the saucepan to a boil.
3. Reduce the heat, and simmer for 10 minutes.
4. Pour into your favorite mugs.
5. Top each with orange peel as garnish, and serve.

- Spiced Hot Chocolate

Drive the winter chill away by savoring this extra special hot drink.

o   Ingredients:

- 12 ounces hot milk
- 1 cup cocoa powder, unsweetened
- 1 cup white sugar
- 2 tablespoons vanilla sugar
- 1 tablespoon ground cinnamon
- ½ teaspoon nutmeg, freshly grated

- ½ teaspoon ground ginger
- ½ teaspoon dried red chili peppers, powdered
- ¼ teaspoon ground cardamom

○ Approximate Prep & Cooking Time: 30 minutes

○ Yield: Makes 12 servings

○ Directions:

1. Sift all ingredients in a mixing bowl.
2. Stir well the ingredients to ensure that they are evenly distributed.
3. Pour the milk into mugs until each is three-fourths full.
4. Stir in 3 tablespoons of the mixture until they have been dissolved.
5. Serve with whipped cream on top, if desired.

Learning how to prepare hyggelig food and beverages means that you can now serve and share these special meals with your loved ones. For many, getting to enjoy the meal with family and friends is enough reason to learn how to cook and bake well. Improving your relationships through good hyggelig food, however, is just one of the many ways to do so. The next chapter discusses how the principles of hygge may be used by parents to foster strong bonds with their children.

Chapter 5

Teaching Children the Principles of Hygge

In Denmark, parents make it a point to inculcate the principles of hygge to their children whenever they can. Such an initiative enables them to raise a new generation of happy, emotionally stable, well-rounded, and resilient individuals who would then apply the same methods to the succeeding generations. It is no wonder then that the Danish people consistently ranks high in happiness surveys conducted in a global scale each year.

The hyggelig way of parenting is not limited by geography or culture though. Anyone who knows its core teachings may be able to achieve the same results as well. Take note, however, that this is not something that you can do overnight. You need to have awareness, patience, resolve, and regular practice in order to reap the benefits of this adopting this parenting style.

If you would recall the numerous benefits of hygge as discussed in an earlier chapter of this book, the time, effort, and resources that you would dedicate for this would be all worth it. Of these benefits, many consider the development of an unbreakable bond between parents and their children to the ultimate motivation for doing so. Therefore, without further do, here are the top parenting strategies and tips that could significantly improve the way you raise your children.

Hyggelig Strategy No. 1: Be a model of authenticity and honesty.

a. Be honest with yourself.

Before you could teach your children to live an authentic life, you must be root out any self-deception that you may have. Having the capacity to recognize and acknowledge different aspects of yourself is an important part of personal growth.

Complete honesty about your emotions and experiences can be hard to achieve. However, striving to reach this state would be of great help in showing your children the value of honesty.

When you are honest with yourself, you can teach them to listen to and express themselves without passing judgment. It would also help them set their moral compasses to the right direction—a feat that is essential in leading an honest life.

b. Respond with honesty.

When your children ask a question, given them a sincere, but age-appropriate and understandable answer. Though they are not aware yet of the concept of non-verbal signal, children tend to be highly intuitive when it comes to lies and deception.

Be honest with your children even when it is hard to do so. Otherwise, you would affect their ability to determine what is right and wrong. Furthermore, when caught in lie, their trust on you as well as their capacity to trust other people would be negatively affected.

c. Refer to your childhood for genuine examples.

Whether it is about the fun times you have had as a child, or about your terrifying first-time visit to the dentist, children could benefit a lot from hearing your actual experiences as a child. It allows them to get to know you better, while also giving them a chance to understand that it is normal to feel happy, sad, or scared, depending on the situation.

d. Improve the quality of your praise.

When it comes to praises, pay attention to the quality, not the quantity. To increase the quality of the praises you give to your children, refer to the pointers given below:

- The most meaningful and beneficial kind of praises are the ones based on the effort rather than the natural abilities of the child.

  Instead of saying, "You are so smart", praise your child by recognizing the hard work that they have put into acing a test—for example, making cue cards, or completing self-review quizzes. Doing so would allow them to learn that perseverance matters in life, not just innate talent and skills.

- Avoid overusing praises.

  Determine if something is worth praising before saying it. If the achievement is too easy, then it would dissuade your children from embracing challenges. Instead, they would settle on things that they think would gain them praise with minimal effort only.

  Do not be too stingy, too. Rather than praising a child for consistently getting an A in a subject, recognize their success but push them to pursue loftier goals, such as increasing the number of subjects wherein they get top marks as well.

- Be sensitive about acknowledging failures or mistakes.

  Expressions such as "You did your best" may sound like pity, so exercise more care when it comes to acknowledging their efforts that did not lead to success. Instead, focus on what they have accomplished at this time, and how they could improve upon themselves to reach their goal. So, for example, you can say this to properly recognize the efforts of your child while motivating them to do better next time: "You may have missed your goal today, but you were so close. Just keep on practicing, so that you would get it right tomorrow."

e. Teach your children to avoid comparing themselves with others.

Comparison leads to competition—a concept that goes against the things that hygge stands for. Not everyone can be the best at everything so it is inevitable that others would be better than you. As such, you would end up feeling resentment, disappointment, and even anger over time.

Eliminate this kind of mindset by making your children to focus on becoming better than their current self. This would encourage them to continue developing their skills and talents, and to keep on doing their best for whatever they are pursuing.

f. Add the phrase "for me" when giving your opinion.

Doing so would show your child that even though your thoughts and feelings differ from theirs, it does not necessarily mean that you are right and that they are wrong.

For example, you are feeding your child hot soup during a cold winter's day. She complained about the soup being too hot, but when you tried it earlier, it was just right for you. Instead of arguing with her or dismissing her complaint as a whimsy of child, say that "Oh, the soup isn't too hot for me. Let me cool it down a bit more, then."

Such a statement shows that you respect their experience, and that you trust their word. This, in turn, would teach them to do the same when faced with similar circumstances later in life.

Hyggelig Strategy No. 2: Foster togetherness with your children.

a. Ask everyone to be in the moment.

Everyone should understand and agree to leave their stresses and worries behind when spending time together. Ask them to avoid dwelling on their negative experiences, and speaking badly of other people. Try to keep things bright and lighthearted because doing so would make the children feel at ease about the idea of socializing with the people they care about.

Remember, too, that children absorb the way you speak and behave. Therefore, if they regularly experience the hyggelig way of togetherness, then they are more likely to do the same with their loved ones later in life.

Some people find it hard to be in the moment. If you are one of these people, then here are some helpful pointer that could get you into the right mindset:

- Visualize the experience that you want to have with your family and friends.
- Equip yourself with healthy coping mechanisms that can calm you down in case you feel stress out later on.

- Make an oath to yourself to avoid conflict and gossip during the gathering.

Staying in the present would also be a lot easier if people would refrain from using personal electronic devices, such as cellphones and tablet PCs. Those things, though helpful in many ways, can be a source of distraction, and could build walls between each other.

b. Having fun as a group should be everyone's goal.

Plan for engaging activities that everyone can participate in. Set aside your personal preferences for now so that you could better think of ways to make things fun for the adults and the children alike.

Encourage everyone to play, but it is best to limit the use of gaming platforms or electronic devices. Arrange for a family playtime that would require them to move around and interact with one another on a personal level.

For a more hyggelig experience, organize activities that promote the idea of working together towards a certain goal. Examples of popular teambuilding activities include scavenger hunts, charades, and building a fort out of pillows and blankets.

Keep things simple though. Too much toys or tasks could distract everyone from the simple things that hygge wants you to appreciate as well. Keep your attention to each other, and when outdoors, take the time every now and then to breathe in the air and take in the scenery around you.

c. Create comfortable meeting places.

Being in the moment, having fun, and building a sense of togetherness would be a more hyggelig experience if done in a cozy environment. Designate places where you would like to gather everyone, such as the living room or the dining room, and make it extra comfortable and relaxing for everyone.

You can do so by setting up ambient lighting around the space, arranging plush seating for everyone, and placing decorations that are appealing and interesting to look at. Remember to prepare good food and beverages to keep everyone satiated and refreshed.

Make sure that your meeting place has enough space for everyone so that they would not feel cramped. This would also be important when it comes to playing games with the kids.

d. Prepare the food and beverage that will be served together.

Invite your children to participate in the preparation for the gathering. Depending on their age, you could assign them simple tasks that would make them feel like they are contributing to the task.

If the food or beverage you are preparing some has history to it, tell them that story as you bond together in the kitchen. This would help them build an appreciation for cooking as well as your family traditions.

e. Refrain from making complaints.

During the gathering, it is likely that you would experience moments that would irritate you, or stress you out. Things might also not come out as you have planned. There are also some things that are out of your control, such as a sudden rain, that could prevent you from doing a supposed activity with your companions.

Rather than voicing out your complaints, and inadvertently putting down the mood, you should try to be more flexible and agile instead. In case it rains while in the middle of playing outside, invite everyone back inside the house, prepare hot drinks, and set a board game that everyone can play instead.

This kind of reaction is vital in teaching the kids how to handle properly handle challenging situations on their own. Most children learn best when shown examples, so be the best model that your children could emulate.

f. Trade stories with them.

Telling stories to a group can be a fun learning experience for kids. Aside from seeing how to share stories with other people, children could benefit also from the lessons that may be gained from the experience of other people.

Happy stories are quite easy to tell for most people. Stories about rough times that have happened to you, on the other hand, could be challenging to share though. Between adults, such stories could be shared so that you could gain advice and support from them.

However, for children, it is best to tell them once you have gotten through those bad times. In simple but honest terms, share with them how you have managed to pushed through those obstacles in your life. Highlight how other people have helped you, too, so that they would also learn the value of reaching out to others, and helping out others in times of need.

Hyggelig Strategy No. 3: Let the children play.

a. Create an environment that is suitable for play.

According to studies on child development, an environment that is stimulating for the senses, such as vision, hearing, and smelling aids in the growth of brain cells among children.

You can set up this kind of setting for your children by sourcing various materials that may be used during playtime. This does not only mean toys, but also art supplies, musical instruments, and other skill-enhancing items.

b. Discourage the use of television and personal electronic devices while playing.

To reap the positive effects of playtime for your child, you must turn off the TV, and take away their access to cellphones, tablets, and other devices. Such items could take their attention away from the supposed play that they are doing.

When allowed to focus, children would be able to use their imagination more effectively. They tend to make up stories that fit into whatever they are doing. If the child is artistically inclined, then the resulting artwork would likely to be more creative and immersive compared to when sources of distraction have not been eliminated.

c. Don't be worry about looking silly when playing with them.

Hygge encourages parents to play with their children to foster a sense of belongingness within the family. When doing so, try to forget about how you would look to other people. Instead, get down to their level, and engage with them wholeheartedly.

Give your children a chance to lead the playtime as well. Support their ideas, and encourage their imagination. You do not have to spend the whole day with them to reap the benefits of playing with your children. Even half an hour per day of playtime would do more wonders than simply buying them a toy.

d. Set aside time for your children to play on their own.

Inviting other kids over for playtime could be extremely hyggelig for your hyggelig. Group plays are also great for the development of the child.

However, studies show that letting a child play by himself/herself could be quite rewarding as well.

According to researchers, when a child is playing alone, he/she is given a chance to develop their own way of processing information. During this activity, the imagination tends to tap more on real-life events that have happened to them. As such, many experts agree that it could be quite therapeutic.

Let the child have a certain level of control over his/her playtime. Try not to intervene too quickly or too much because it would help them develop resilience. Take a step back, and watch as they learn some of the most important skills that they need to live a happy life.

e. Supply your children with art materials.

Let your children try hand at creating art on their own. Give them a nice variety, and allow them to pick the ones that they enjoy the most. It is fine to show them at first how to make art using a particular set of materials. However, after they have gotten the hang of it, let them make something out of their own imagination.

Remember to display your children's artwork, too. This would show that you value their talent and hard work. If they find this experience as fun and rewarding for themselves, then they might be interested in pursuing it as a serious skill.

f. Allow your children to explore the outdoors.

Make plans for your children to play outside of your home. For an even more hyggelig experience, the best places to go to are the woods and the beach. If such trips are impractical, then the local park would do as well.

When heading outdoors, research first about the safety of the areas that you planning to go to. If a place is safe enough, then the children may be allowed to explore the area without much risk involved. This kind of activity would enable them to use their imagination while forming a connection with nature.

Hyggelig Strategy No. 4: Teach the children the value of empathy.

a. Take the time to discover and understand your personal empathic style first.

By doing so, you would be able to better impart the value of empathy to your children. Moreover, it can be extremely hard to teach something that you do not personally know.

Here are some guide questions that could help you get started on this. Remember, it is not enough to just think and reflect upon these points. You must also aim to become more self-aware, and then observe how you truly act. Invite your partner to do so as well. You belong to the same team, and therefore, should have similar levels of understanding. In this way, your chances of achieving your goal of teaching empathy to your children would become significantly higher.

- What does empathy mean for you?
- How does your partner think of empathy?
- Which points do you and your partner agree, and where do you disagree?
- How much judgment do you impose to yourself and to other people?
- How judgmental is your partner towards others?
- In what way does this affect your words and your manner of speaking?

If you have observed yourself to be exhibiting judgment towards other people, think of ways on how you can change your ways for the better.

Figuring out how you could be more empathic towards yourself and others is necessary because your children would likely pick up your language and mannerisms. The same applies for your partner. Strive to be better at expressing empathy so that your children can mirror your good values and practices.

b. Try to see things from the perspective of other people.

When interacting with another individual, try to always practice this rather than giving into your biases and assumptions. Avoid shaming others because that would give them a reason to find ways to defend themselves from you.

Putting yourself in their shoes would enable you to practice empathy, and thus become more skillful at it in the same process. Over time and with regular practice, you would be able to show your children the proper way of exhibiting empathy instead of just telling them how.

c. Guide your children on how to observe and identify the emotions of others without judgment.

As an adult, it is tempting to label things as you see them since it is quicker and easier to do so than taking the time to understand the reactions and feelings of other people. Children are even more susceptible to this.

Given this, you must carefully guide them through the process of recognizing the emotions of the people around them. For instance, your child told you that one of his classmates screamed out of anger while playing with the other children during their break time at school.

Instead of just saying that his classmate should not have done so because it is improper to scream and be angry with others, ask your child these questions to help him understand the situation and prevent him from making quick judgments about others:

- Did you see what happened to your classmate that made him scream?
- Can you describe to me what happened to your classmate?
- Why do you think that made your classmate scream?
- How do you feel after seeing your classmate scream?
- Why do you feel that way?

As you can see, these questions do not attempt to jump right away to the emotions at play during the situation. It starts by instilling the importance of getting the details right before making an analysis. Then, the succeeding question prods the child to think from the perspective of others, and then themselves.

By answering the first two questions, the child would have gained a better grasp of what happened. When done right, this could help your child reach an understanding of his own emotions and those of others.

d. Encourage your children to read.

According to studies, reading books to young children helps in significantly increasing their capacity for empathy. However, this does not mean that you only have to limit yourself to books with positive and lighthearted themes.

Experts in child develop encourages the act of reading books with negative emotions and reactions, such as sadness, grief, anger, and loneliness, to children in order to make them better understand the world they live in. They do, however, advise caution, sensitivity, and patience when explaining the said themes to young minds.

In the long run, this practice gives the children the right foundation in handling difficult situations and negative emotions. Since they been taught in a well-rounded manner, they would be able to gain an empathic side that they could apply in different aspects of their lives later on.

e. Show the children how to improve upon the meaningful relationships you have with other people.

In life, it is inevitable that you would have strained or fractured relationships with the people who matter to you. Patching things up between you and them is a good way of exhibiting to your children the importance of empathy.

Studies show that a certain part of the brain is responsible for both empathy and forgiveness. Therefore, the higher your level of empathy is, the more likely you are to forgive other people.

Mending the meaningful relationships in your life bears great importance because this would influence your general happiness. As such, practicing empathy and learning how to forgive would improve the quality of your life. Teach your children this lesson in order to better motivate them to embrace these values throughout their lives.

f.   Feel free to show your children your vulnerable side.

As you listen to your children, do not worry about coming across as vulnerable, especially when giving them advice. Showing them that it is okay to express their feelings and show how much they care would prompt them to do the same.

Be deliberate about this, however. Your goal is to impart true empathy to your children, not reckless emotions and words that you cannot easily take back.

As a final note, children are raised not just by their parents, but also by other family members and friends. Choosing to surround yourself with individuals who place great importance on honesty, togetherness, creativity, and empathy would help you in teaching the said values to your children.

Chapter 6

Improving Work Performance and Satisfaction Through Hygge

The practice of hygge goes beyond the home and yourself. It can also be used to enhance the working environment to promote collaboration, productivity, and wellbeing of the employees.

How is this possible?

As explained earlier, hygge is not just about buying things that are associated with, or arranging the office in a certain way. You do not see a hyggelig workplace, but rather feel it day by day. As such, it makes people want to go to work every single day. The reason for working is not solely about earning money, but also because they enjoy what they are doing.

When work satisfaction is high, it creates an atmosphere that is conducive for the achievement of the following:

- Wellbeing of the employees

  Several organizations that are considered as leaders of their respective fields recognize the value of ensuring the wellbeing of their employees. Aside from preventing them from being overly fatigued and vulnerable to sickness, the improvement of employees' wellbeing contributes to their ability to produce more creative and innovative output. Furthermore, studies show that placing a high value on wellbeing enables the organization to retain its employees for a longer period of time, and dissuades them from thinking of leaving the organization for a competitor.

Given these benefits, many businesses nowadays seek for ways to understand how they could foster the wellbeing of their respective employees. Experts point them to various strategies, one of which is the concept of hygge.

How exactly does a hyggelig workspace enhance the wellbeing of employees?

o   Physical Wellbeing

Experts in workspace design recommend the provision for seats and desks that allows various types of posture. Requiring the employees to just sit down while they work can be particularly detrimental to their health. As such, the workplace must include furniture that may be used while standing up or lounging about as well.

This is where hygge comes into play.

- It promotes the idea of using plush couches, soft armchairs, and cozy mats, which the employees may use depending on the kind of work that they are doing. Some businesses refrain from assigning dedicated workstations to each employee so that anyone could pick the seating that would make them feel more at ease and focused.

- For those who prefer standing up, desks that may adjusted accordingly are also highly encouraged. Rather than metal or plastic desks, hygge encourages the use of wooden desks for a more authentic feel that also elevates the aesthetics of the workplace.

- Letting in natural light from the outside does not only benefit businesses by contributing to the conservation of energy, but it also decreases the stress levels of the employees, while making them feel more energized throughout the day.

- Pantry areas enables the employees to socialize while they eat their meals together. Hygge preaches the value of eating with other people, not just because it wants you to be more social, but also because communal eating could lead to the adoption of healthier eating habits exhibited by those around you.

- Some employers offer special perks for their employees. These are not the kind of benefits that are not required by law nor are commonly given by a lot of businesses. Popular examples of such perks include free on-site massage, and comfortable sleeping pods.

o Cognitive Wellbeing

A hyggelig workspace enhances the ability of the employees to concentrate on their work, while also giving them spaces where they can rest and rejuvenate at some point during the work day. Organizations create this kind of workspaces by:

- Placing live plants across different parts of the office.

Hygge wants you to form a strong connection with nature, but it can be hard to do so when you have to work for most of the day. Some organizations provide their employees this opportunity by taking inspirations from nature for their interior decoration.

This does not mean having to spend thousands of dollars just to turn the office green. One of the simplest and most hyggelig ways to do so is by setting up parts of the workplace dedicated for the live plants. Depending on the level of commitment and the available space that may be allocated for it, this may be done by creating a mini garden somewhere in the premises, or by arranging potted plants around the office.

Either method works effectively in producing the intended positive effect on the mental wellbeing of the employees. The sight of natural greens could help alleviate stress and tension, as well as fatigue.

Studies also show that workspaces that feature plants tend to have employees with increased capacity to concentrate on their respective tasks for an extended period of time.

- Playing music in the background.

Employees, especially those that work in a production line, may be able to produce more and higher quality output when the right kind of tune is played in the background. Music helps them get into the ideal rhythm that is best suited to their kind of work.

Music can be extremely hyggelig when it inspires positive feelings among those who listen to it. Aside from increasing productivity, certain types of music can calm down a stressed out individual, or provide the right ambience for relaxing both the body and mind.

Given the benefits of music, a growing number of businesses are looking into how they could better harness the hyggelig qualities of music for the betterment of their employees.

- Applying the ideal palette for improved cognitive performance on the interiors of the office.

Color psychology points out the propensity of the human mind to be significantly affected by colors. Studies show that with the right set of colors, an employee's quality of work, productivity, and general mood may be significantly improved.

Hygge is not associated with a specific color, but it encourages you to connect with nature. Therefore, the best way to reap the benefits from both color psychology and hygge is to apply colors that may be found in nature to the workspace.

For your reference, here are the suggested hyggelig colors and their respective effects on job performance:

- Blue
  - Calms the mind
  - Lowers heart rate and blood pressure
  - Fosters communication and trust

Given these effects, blue is best applied for areas used for brainstorming with the team.

- Yellow
  - Promotes optimistic feelings and mindset
  - Provides a boost of energy
  - Stimulate the mind to think

Due to said effects, you should consider using yellow as an accent only since too much of it may agitate the employees' temper and anxiety. However, if you are intent on making this as the primary color, then apply it for workspaces that are used for coming up with creative and innovative ideas.

- Green

  - Increases creativity
  - Inspires innovative thinking
  - Reduces anxiety
  - Prevents eye strain
  - Fosters balance and harmony

  Since green has powerful yet calming effects, it is best applied for offices that mainly relies on computers for daily operations.

- White

  - Makes the workspace look spacious
  - Boosts creativity

  The blank slate the white presents stimulates the mind to come up with creative ideas. Hence, it is best used for areas where employees create plans and designs.

o Emotional Wellbeing

Aside from assuring the physical and mental wellbeing of the employees, it is also important and beneficial, in the long run, to care for their emotional stability. Through this, they would be able to feel more at ease with their superiors, teammates, and subordinates.

There are various ways to ensure the emotional wellbeing of employees. Here are the top recommendations that you should consider doing at work:

- Spend your lunch break outdoors

  Some employees feel obliged to eat their lunch in their workstations so that they can stay on top to catch important emails as they arrive, or so that they can make plans for their next projects. Having this kind of habit can be abrasive not only to your cognitive performance, but also for your emotional wellbeing.

  Studies show that employees who do so tend to have increased stress levels, thus decreasing their control over their emotions as well as their capacity to handle tough situations later in the day. Since they have not taken the time to recharge themselves properly, their work performance still suffers despite their intention to be more productive at work.

To keep you from making the same mistake, you should practice the hyggelig way of eating your lunch during a workday. Since you are not likely able to go home and have lunch with your family, the next best option is to go outside, and eat your lunch on your own or with your co-workers.

You may walk to the nearest deli, and buy a nice sandwich and a tumbler of fresh fruit juice for lunch. If you prefer preparing and packing your food, then bring it with you to the nearest park, and eat it there.

While outside, remember to unwind both your body and mind as well. Breathe in some fresh air. If the weather is pleasant, then appreciate the feeling of sunlight against your skin. Forget about what tasks you have to work on when you get back from your break. Just focus in the moment, and enjoy your time away from your desk.

- Personalize your desk or workstation

  Most people spend the majority of their day in the office, so it is best to turn it into something that feels like home. Offices nowadays are more lenient when it comes to the decoration of the individual workspaces of their employees.

  Unless you work in a manufacturing company or a laboratory, then you likely enjoy a higher degree of freedom when it comes to bringing in some personal items that may be used for decorating your workspace. If you have not yet thought about doing this, then here are some good ideas that you may want to try for yourself:

  - Framed pictures of your family and friends
  - Souvenirs from memorable vacations
  - A collection of different tea leaves kept in a nice wooden box
  - Scented candles, if permitted by the company

- A bouquet of your favorite flowers placed in a vase
- An artwork made by you, a family member, or a friend

Using such items for upgrading your desk or workstation can make you feel cozier at work. When you are stressed out, you may just look at them, and reflect about their meaning or the memories attached to them. Eventually, you will feel calmer and more energized again, ready to take on the rest of your work day.

- Give sincere recognition to the employees

As explained earlier, hygge is not just about turning your workplace into a cozy spot, or spending your lunch break with your co-workers. It is also about creating a working environment where the employees feel appreciated.

Expressing sincerity through encouraging words and gestures helps in reducing stress levels and lifting up the employees' spirits. Such kindness also increases their resilience, thus enabling them to push through even when faced with various challenges during the work day.

When a culture of sincere recognition has been established, the employees themselves would gradually help it grow and spread across the workplace. Performing random acts of kindness as a way of paying it forward would become more common each day. As a result, hygge may be felt and experienced by everyone and anywhere within the workplace.

- Collaboration among the employees

Hygge supports the collaboration of employees by promoting activities and set-ups that encourages openness, kindness, and communication. Traditional means of achieving this, like conducting daily briefings and assigning the employees into group projects, could only work to some level. Bringing them closer to one another on a much deeper level requires the application of hyggelig principles on the day to day operations of the business.

Below are some great ideas that your HR specialists would definitely agree with:

o   Organize or attend teambuilding activities

Embracing the spirit of teamwork is an integral step of achieving a hyggelig workspace. As such, employers should give importance to exercises that enhance the sense of belongingness of the employees among each other.

Teambuilding activities take time to plan and execute, however. To give you a head-start on this, here are some excellent ideas that are aligned with the principles of hygge:

  ▪   Watersports Activities

Most companies include going to the beach as one of their planned teambuilding activities. That by itself is hyggelig since it enables the employees to spend time with each other while enjoying the sun, sand, and waves. To further elevate it though, you should also consider doing watersports in the itinerary.

It does not have to be as extreme as riding jet skis or surfing, nor does it have to be held at beaches only. If there is a nearby river or lake, then head there for a day of paddling a canoe, kayaking, or even sports fishing. Such activities promote collaboration among the employees while bringing them even closer to nature.

- Karaoke Nights

  Several companies find this as one of the simplest yet fun ways to foster camaraderie among the employees. It is quite easy to arrange a karaoke night these days because you can just either place a reservation at a karaoke bar, or set it up on your own with just a smart TV, speakers, and microphones.

  Through karaoke nights, the employees would get a chance to relax and have fun while discovering the hidden talents of their co-workers. Furthermore, song choices are excellent sources of conversation, especially when you find others who have the same taste in music as you.

- Room Escape Challenges

  Room escape games have become more popular over the recent years. They are not just for recreational fun with your family and friends though. HR specialists have recognized this type of activity as an excellent way of honing the leadership abilities, patience, creative thinking, and teamwork of the employees.

If you are not familiar with this, a room escape challenge involves locking up a group of people inside a room for a particular period of time. Within the said limit, the group must find clues and solve puzzles in order to set themselves free.

Without a strong collaboration among the participants, this activity could be especially hard or even impossible to do. As such, including room escape challenges in your annual teambuilding plans is highly recommended for every organization.

- Volunteering for local institutions

For an even more beneficial use of time, teambuilding activities may be combined with volunteer work. The latter is usually just categorized under the corporate social responsibility (CSR) of the company.

However, inviting the employees to take part in this could inspire them to connect better with each other while providing assistance to those in need.

Common examples of volunteer work that may be turned into a teambuilding exercise include:

- ➢ Feeding the homeless during the holidays
- ➢ Providing on-site assistance to institutions for people with special needs
- ➢ Distributing gifts at a children's hospital

Involving your employees with CSR activities of the company also increases the success of these initiatives. Studies also show that, when conducted regularly, these activities enhance the emotional wellbeing of the employees.

o Invite your co-workers for a potluck party in your home

Good food eaten along with other people exemplifies some of the best values that are associated with hygge. Since this kind of lifestyle also promotes the idea of frugal living, you may save up on cash by hosting a potluck dinner for your colleagues rather than going out with them to restaurants or bars.

A potluck differs from a regular dinner party because of this important requirement: every participant must contribute at least one dish—typically home-cooked—that may be shared among everyone attending the party. Instead of just one or two persons being responsible for the food, everyone gets to prepare something special that they want others to enjoy as well.

Conversations during a potluck party could also be a lot more interesting because you may discover who among your co-workers have hidden talents when it comes to cooking or baking. Furthermore, people usually prepare something special for potlucks—such as recipes that have been passed within the families. Bringing up these topics during the dinner enables everyone to get to know each other better, thereby fostering deeper and stronger bonds that are essential for more effective collaborations at work.

o Set up shared working spaces for the employees

   Open layouts do not only apply for houses. Offices may also benefit greatly from the reduction of closed offices and the usage of cubicles.

   To give the employees even more opportunity to collaborate with one another, place tables and chairs around the office that can accommodate at least four persons. In this way, they will have spaces that could be used for group work and brainstorming sessions. Facilitate the flow of ideas by providing them portable drawing boards and markers, as well as projectors or screens.

Hygge has originally been developed by the Danish people to combat the harsh conditions they experience during wintertime. Nowadays, it is no longer just limited to cold, dark nights. Its scope continues to widen as people continually discover ways of introducing hygge to different aspects of life, including the workplace.

Happiness, comfort, and security may not be the first things you think of when asked about the best ways to increase the productivity and creativity of the employees. However, as exhibited by the Danes and the various studies conducted about the effects of working in a hyggelig workplace, it has been proven that bringing in the comforts and familiarity of a home to the workplace ensures the overall wellness of the employees, and enhances the way they collaborate with one another. These two points contribute significantly to the employee's work satisfaction—which is considered as one of the key factors that brings the performance and profitability of the company to even greater heights.

Chapter 7

Experiencing Hygge All Year Long

Many people believe that winter, particularly Christmastime, is the peak of hygge. After all, when people think of the things they want to do during this season, their ideas are centered around activities that would make them feel warm and cozy—for example, intimate get-togethers and thoughtful exchanges of gifts.

If you know the kind of winter that Danes usually have, their heavy reliance on hygge to get them through the cold and dreary season would make so much sense.

Each year, Denmark experiences one month wherein the nights are far longer than the days. During this time, feeling a bit of sunshine on your skin becomes a luxury that only the few lucky ones get to enjoy. This prolonged darkness and extreme cold could make anyone feel miserable and even sickly.

Fortunately, the Danes have developed an effective way to combat the horrible aspects of winter. Rather than succumbing to the harsh realities of this season, they make the best out of what they have by practicing hygge whenever they get the chance to do so.

Though hygge is something that you can do any time of the year, it is during winter that it becomes a daily necessity for those living in Denmark. Without it, celebrating the holidays would be nearly impossible. Imagine spending Christmas eve without a thick sweater or a mug of steaming hot chocolate. Watching the carolers outside would not be as enjoyable if your home feel just as cold as the outside.

Christmas and hygge go hand in hand for the Danes, so naturally they even have a distinct term for it—julehygge. This term, which translates to "Christmas hygge", can be used as a noun, a verb and an adjective.

Though Denmark has mostly the same Christmas traditions as with other European nations, there is something different about how they prepare for and spend this holiday due to their disposition for anything hygge. To achieve the right atmosphere for enjoying julehygge, here is the perfect recipe that you may want to follow:

- Companionship

  In Denmark, thousands of people usually move to Copenhagen, its capital, for more diverse work opportunities. However, during Christmastime, these same people migrate back to their hometowns so they could spend the holidays with their family and friends. Given this, you may say that julehygge starts and ends in the company of the people you care about.

On a normal day, you most likely spend more time either at work, at school, or somewhere else other than your home. As such, you get to see too little of the people you value the most in the world. Fortunately, the time freed up before and after the holidays makes Christmas the perfect opportunity to make up for this.

Spending quality time with your loved ones is one of the hallmark traits of hygge. Therefore, celebrating the holidays with your family and friends contributes to the achievement of julehygge. You can fully attain it through good food, festive decors, and fun social activities.

- Food

Danish Christmas would not be complete without authentic and carefully prepared meals for you and your loved ones. During this time of the year, the main dish consists of roasted meat. Most people prefer either duck or pork—some have even crafted recipes that combines both.

To balance out the meat, the Danes also serve boiled or caramelized potatoes, as well as pickled gherkins, stewed cabbage, and lots of gravy. Some households pair their meats with different types of bread for variety.

As a final touch, a unique Danish dessert called risalamande brings in a much needed sweetness to the meal. It is made of equal parts of rice and whipped cream, with minced almonds thrown in. Cherry sauce is drizzled on top to make it look festive. Since Christmas dinner in Denmark is a social affair, risalamande is served in a large bowl that is shared among the guests.

To make it even more fun, the Danes play a game using a whole almond placed somewhere in the bowl of risalamande. Whoever gets the almond wins a special prize, and earns plenty of praises for being lucky from the other guests. This combination of good food and a lighthearted game exhibit the dedication of the Danes to the art of hygge.

- Decors

To properly celebrate julehygge, you must put up Christmas decorations around your home. In Denmark, it is common for older generations to hand down their collection of decors to the younger ones. These include classic Christmas figurines of Father Christmas, elves, and reindeers. Those who are more religiously inclined also have decorations based on the Nativity scene of the Bible.

Woven hearts crafted from glossy colored paper are also popular in Denmark during Christmastime. According to historians, this traditional decoration originated from the master storyteller Hans Christian Andersen, who excels at creating paper cuttings.

It would not be a hyggelig Christmas without lighting up your home with candles. As mentioned earlier, Denmark experiences long, cold nights during winter. Candles and other sources of ambient lighting brings in a warm glow that bathes everything and everyone inside.

Candles are also involved in a Danish tradition that bears similarities with the practice of lighting up Christmas candles. The Danes call it the advent candle, and it features markings on the side bearing the dates from December 1 up to December 24.

Every day, the Danes light up the candle until it has melted up to the point corresponding to the current date. This is usually done either in the early morning or in the evening, just before the family eats their supper.

When placed in the dinner table, the advent candle serves as the main centerpiece. It reminds everyone of the number of days left before Christmas, while functioning as an additional source of light. This inclusion of the advent candle to dinnertime showcases another instance wherein the Danes combine social activities with other aspects of their lives.

Lighting up the candle every day is just one of the many activities that the Danish people to countdown the days before Christmas day. For example:

o   Advent Calendar

Children are given advent calendars that they could flip through to mark the passing days until Christmas day itself. Each page contains a distinctive Christmas icon or motif so that children could also learn more about the holidays.

o   Julekalender

TV stations broadcast their own julekalender from December 1 to 24. Julekalender refers to a series of Christmas-themed stories that are geared mostly for kids. The stories progress each day, and reaches a climax by the 24th.

Besides educating the children about Christmas, julekalender also helps out the adults by keeping the children engaged while they make last-minute preparations for Christmas day.

Aside from Christmas activities, the Danes practice winter hygge through knitting. Many consider this as one of the ultimate hyggelig activities that one can do, especially when it is cold.

Knitting can be quite relaxing for the body and calming for the mind. It sends out signals that everything is well, and that nothing else needs to be attended to immediately. Plus, by the end of this activity, you would get to have a new sweater, mittens, hat, gloves, or socks, which you could use for yourself, or for gifting to those you care about. Those thick, fluffy, and carefully woven clothing pieces would give you extras doses of hygge for the cold season.

Practicing Hygge During Springtime

Extreme cold is not a prerequisite for the practice of hygge. Springtime could be still hyggelig when you slow down, and celebrate the return of the warmer months with your family and friends.

To do so, here are some great ideas that you should try doing once the long winter nights have ended:

a. Join or create your own community garden.

Doing this activity would inspire an uptrend in hygge on a bigger scale. Nowadays, you can find at least one community garden per town or city. If there is none near you, then you can ask permission from the local government to start one. It is also advisable to get other people on board this early on, so you could get their help with the plans and initial funding for the project.

There are plenty of benefits that could make this initiative worth your while. Studies show that taking care of plants can be relaxing for the body and mind. Since you are going to do it with other people, you would also be able to connect with other people and nature. As such, it can be both meditative and hyggelig for everyone participating in it.

b. Go cycling.

Aside from candles and Lego, the Danes are widely known for their love of cycling. They use their bikes when they go to work, to school, or for running errands. Recreational cycling, especially in summer, is arguably the most hyggelig of these, however.

Using a bicycle for whatever purpose lets you enjoy the sun and breeze as you speed along the streets. It gets the blood pumping without overly exhausting you in the process. It does not emit gases that are harmful for both the body and the environment. Ultimately, cycling makes people feel happier and healthier.

c. Practice drawing or painting outdoor scenes.

During springtime, trees and flowers begin to regain their vibrancy and beauty after a long cold season. Simply watching this happen can be a hyggelig experience, but it would be a lot more rewarding if you would capture this in a drawing or a painting.

Remember to invite your family and friends, too. Prepare a nice picnic with cheeses, fresh fruit, and wine to turn this into a cultured but relaxing experience.

Hygge Living During Summer

Though summer is not exactly the season for candles and hot chocolate, it can be filled with hygge, too.

For many, summer means tanned skin, swimming, and lots of sunscreen. It can also mean warm nights spent by grilling barbecue, and drinking beer with your family and friends.

The kind of activities that you plan for summer might be totally different compared to those you want to do during winter, but that does not mean that those activities are going to be devoid of hygge. As long as you are doing things that make you feel warm, comfortable, and connection with other people and nature, then you would be experiencing a hyggelig summer.

For your guidance, here are top 5 recommended activities that you should definitely try doing next summer:

a. Pick fruits at an orchard.

Spending the day at an orchard to pick fruits from the trees is extremely hyggelig. You can choose any kind of orchard, but in Denmark, apple orchards are the most popular ones.

Once you have gather enough fruits, you may to block off your schedule for the following day in order to turn the fresh fruits into jams or sweet preserves. Others also make use of certain fruits for making special cider.

b. Invite your family and friends for a barbecue.

Grilling meat and sausages over open fire is one of the widely practiced hyggelig activity across the world. Barbecue has a universal quality, wherein almost every culture has its own version of it.

To make it more pleasant, throw a barbecue party with the people you care about. Make sure to get a nice variety of meat and vegetables for everyone's enjoyment.

c. Have a picnic by the beach.

The beach is not just for swimming or sunbathing. It can also be a great site for a picnic with your loved ones.

Summer ushers in the peak season for farmers' market. As such, you may be able to get a nice selection of fresh fruits, cheeses, and breads for a bountiful picnic. Make it even more hyggelig by preparing a thick, fluffy blanket where you and your companions can lay into while chatting, eating, and relaxing at the beach.

Welcoming Autumn the Hygge Way

During fall, the temperature starts dropping once more until it finally gives way to another winter season. You might think that this would dampen everyone's spirit, but as you may have observed, autumn is one of the more festive seasons for many people.

Those who practice hygge would likely agree with this. As the nights starts to grow longer and colder, they also begin to spend more time indoors, cuddling and relaxing by the fire together with family and friends. To make this season extra hyggelig, here are some top recommendations for you:

a. Bake special treats for your family and friends.

Freshly baked goods, such as cakes, cookies, and breads, can be made extra special if you would personally bake them for yourself and for your loved ones.

The act of baking itself tends to be therapeutic. Kneading a dough, and watching it rise could be quite satisfying, even without having to taste yet the results of your hard work.

Serve these baked treats when you have invited over some company, or wrap them up nicely so that you can give them as gifts for the people you care about.

b. Go to a sauna.

A sauna, or also known as sudatory, is a place where you can relax your body and mind through controlled heat sessions. The Danes, in particular, are known for having a weekly trip to the sauna so that they can unwind and recharge themselves.

Going to a sauna during autumn is extremely hyggelig, especially when you also use your time there to reflect about the people, things, and experiences that you feel grateful for. Remember to keep yourself hydrated though, especially when you plan to stay long inside the sauna.

c. Capture autumnal scenes through pictures.

In countries that experience the full colors of fall, foliage tours are quite popular activities for the locals and tourists alike. This activity involves exploring areas, typically forests and mountains, where the leaves are beginning or have already changed colors.

During a foliage tour, take the time to look for the most beautiful spots that you would want to capture through a camera. Aside from preserving the memory, these pictures could serve as your way of bringing in a part of nature into your home or workplace. Frame the photos that you have taken, and display them somewhere that you could see whenever you feel tired or stressed out. The golden colors of autumn, along with the memories of your experience back then, could help soothe your body, mind, and spirit.

Based on these suggestions, you can easily practice and experience hygge all year round. You are not limited to these examples though. As long as you can turn something into a joyful, warm, or cozy occasion, then it would be considered a hyggelig activity.

Another important thing to keep in mind is to keep things simple as much as you can. You do not have to spend a lot of money in order to practice hygge through the different seasons of the year. Turn your focus on your feelings from doing a particular activity rather than the opinions of other people about you.

To learn more about how the practice of hygge could actually save you money in the long run, proceed to the next chapter.

Chapter 8

Enjoying a Frugal Life
Through Hyggelig Practices

There is an old saying that goes, "The best things in life are free." Hygge promotes this belief because you do not have to buy expensive things or hoard a lot of stuff just to feel happiness and comfort.

Experts in hygge living know that hygge is far from luxury. It is quite humble and low-key since it encourages simplicity over opulence, and ambience over intensity. There is nothing rich about swaddling yourself with a fleece blanket, or savoring a cup of hot lemon tea, but both of those things are extremely hyggelig.

Here are ten great suggestions that show how the practice of hygge can lead to a frugal living:

1. Have fun with the whole group by playing board games.

   Compared to popular digital forms of entertainment, such as mobile games and streaming apps, board games are considered as more hyggelig. When you play a game on your phone, regardless of whether it is a social game or not, the time you can spend for a personal interaction with other people is going to be significantly lessened.

Instead of just facing a screen, board games can be just as fun while keeping things hygge for you and your companions. Variety would not likely be an issue because there is a wide array of board games available nowadays.

Other than the intimate touch that board games can provide, they can also bring forth nostalgic feelings for simpler and slower times. Hours may pass by without anyone noticing since everyone is having a great time.

2. Throw a pantry party with your family and friends.

A pantry party is a cheap and novel way of having fun with your loved ones. The rules are quite easy to follow, too.

a. Every participant must bring along with him/her the ingredients of something that can be stocked in a pantry or in the fridge—for example, chicken stock, vegetable soup, fruit jams, sauces, or even doughs.

b. Every participant should also bring their own containers that would be appropriate and sufficient for the items that will be prepared.

c. The participants will prepare, cook, and pack together the said pantry items.

d. Divide the finished goods among the participants.

By the end of this activity, you would not just have a batch of the goods you have prepared yourself. You would end up with a set of homemade pantry items that you would normally have to either prepare on your own or buy from the store. As such, you would not only be saving up on money, but also on time and effort.

3. Designate a TV/movie night every week.

Reserve at least one night each week for watching your favorite TV shows, or the movies that have caught your interest. You might be tempted to binge watch everything, especially in the age of streaming apps, but spacing out your viewings can turn a solitary activity into a fun hangout with your friends.

This can be much cheaper than going to theaters since popcorn, soda, and other popular snacks are usually a lot more expensive than buying them from the supermarket, and preparing them on your own.

Furthermore, watching TV and movies in the comforts of your own home feels a lot more hyggelig than sitting in a cold room that sometimes smell weird.

4. Ride a bicycle whenever applicable.

   Cycling has a lot of benefits that goes beyond the body and the mind—it is already generally a lot cheaper than driving a vehicle, or using public transportation.

   Going to work, running errands, or simply exploring the city—ride a bike for short trips that does not require carrying around a lot of baggage. You may install a basket, of course, but that would only be enough for a medium-sized bag of goods or supplies at most.

5. Create a mini library.

   Encourage your neighbors to help you form a mini library that will be shared by all. Gather up the books that you have lying around your home, and ask the others to the same. Set aside a dedicated space for the books, and arrange them in an orderly fashion.

When everything is set up, establish a rule wherein the borrower would have to leave a book whenever they want to borrow one from the library. In this way, you would maintain the number of books while increasing its diversity. You would also get to enjoy new titles without having to buy it on your own.

For a more hyggelig experience, put comfortable couches and armchairs in the library so that visitors would have a place where they could hangout and read together.

6. Attend outdoor film screenings.

   Outdoor cinemas are quite popular during summertime in several cities. Compared to watching movies in traditional theaters, doing it outside tends to be cheaper, but still fun way to spend time with your loved ones, friends, and family.

   To make this a hyggelig outing, you should make the most of its less formal setting. Spending hours out in an open field and under the stars could be quite relaxing or romantic, depending on who you are with. You can also bring along food and drinks with you so that you can have a mini picnic while watching the movie.

Do not forget to bring along some cushions where you and your companions can sit and lounge about. Some prefer bringing plastic chairs, but that could get uncomfortable when used for an extended period of time. Using chairs may also get in the way of other people's viewing experience.

When the film ends, you and your companions may stay for a bit longer to talk about each other's thoughts about the plot, acting, and other aspects of the movie. Listen well and share your opinions with the people with you to keep the conversion lively and meaningful.

7. Swap gifts using current belongings that are no longer in use.

Do you have something in your basement that you have stored there for future use, but have never had a reason to bring it out again since then? Or perhaps someone has given you an electric kettle as a gift but you already have one in the first place. Rather than waiting for the occasion where you may find some use for it, why not invite your family and friends for a simple gathering where you can all swap items that you are not using at all?

Such parties can be quite hyggelig because of all the good spirit and fun times that it could bring for everyone participating in it. You might think that you could just sell the stuff on a garage sale, a flea market, or somewhere in the Internet. However, none of those options can provide you a hyggelig experience at all.

If you are interested in doing a swap party with your family and friends, follow the steps given below:

a. Every participant must bring something that he/she does not use anymore, but may have some value for other people. This could be a piece of furniture, lighting, décor, appliances, or even electronic devices. Some prefer swapping clothes with one another, but that could be trickier because of the probable size difference among the participants.

b. During the party, everyone should be given time to describe the item they wish to swap with something else. You may want to talk about how you got it in the first place, why you are no longer using it, and what you are hoping to get in exchange for it.

c. Once everyone has been given the chance to speak, commence the swapping. Do it one person at a time to avoid creating unnecessary chaos. It is normal for at least two people to want the same thing. In such instances, let them have enough time to talk it out to determine who should ultimately get the item.

Other than getting something that would be useful for you, a swap party would help you clear out your home of the unnecessary stuff that you have in there. A clean home with minimal clutter is considered as a prerequisite for a home filled with hygge.

8. Complete DIY projects.

Challenge yourself with DIY projects that you may then use for decorating your home or workstation, or for gifting to your loved ones. In comparison to pre-made ones that are normally sold in shops, DIY items tend to be much, much cheaper. However, take note that you do have to invest your time instead in order to turn a project into a success.

Aside from nifty little trinkets and artworks, try to create homemade beauty products from scratch. Just make sure to research for a recipe that comes with a guarantee from others, and that you could easily follow.

If you are not willing to risk your hair or skin given your skills at DIY projects, then opt to make your own cleaning supplies instead. With the right set of ingredients and well-written instructions, you may be able to produce dishwashing liquids, stain removers, smell absorbers, and other helpful home supplies that also come with your favorite scents.

DIY clothing projects can be quite hyggelig, too. Normally, people do this by knitting sweaters, scarves, and other garments that are ideal for the cold season. However, you are free to try other sewing or weaving techniques that would better suit your skill level and personal style.

9. Make smarter purchases.

Frugal living does not mean that you have to settle for whatever is the cheapest. Instead, it requires you to be smarter when it comes to evaluating whether or not you should purchase a particular item. Through this, you may be assured that you are getting the best value for your money.

Hygge also promotes the quality over quantity in everything that you do. Therefore, instead of buying something that would break after a couple of uses—this prompting you to purchase a replacement—opt for something that could last for a longer period of time, even with regular use.

Finding, saving, and using coupons for purchases could help you save money, too. Through these, you would either keep yourself from paying the full price, or get you an extra item for a lesser price—or sometimes, for free!

Keep in mind though that the usage of coupons, as well as purchasing a discounted item, could only be considered as a sign of frugal living if the item you wish to buy is something that you really need or want. If your reason for buying it is mainly due to the supposed savings that you would get from doing so, then what you are doing runs against the principles of hygge.

10. Learn how to repair and maintain things that you frequently use.

Equipping yourself with this kind of skills would help you save a lot of money every year. Since learning how to do major repairs could take a lot of time, you should focus first on figuring out how to troubleshooting and doing minor repairs and maintenance works for things like:

- o Your car, motorcycle, or bicycle
- o The plumbing of your house
- o Replacement of batteries for smoke detectors
- o Sanding and repainting of walls or cabinets
- o Installing different types of locks on doors

Nowadays, many people tap online tutorials and videos for instructions on how to do this. However, since hygge encourages you to spend time with other people, you may ask for guidance from a family member, a friend, or a co-worker who is knowledgeable about this. Turn the lessons into a bonding time with them, and remember to express your gratitude afterwards.

Frugal living based on hyggelig principles is not about depriving yourself. Instead, it is about becoming more resourceful so that you may still enjoy your favorite things in life without having to spend so much money for it. It about finding out creative ways to save money so that you could truly enjoy your days once you have retired from work, or so that you could achieve your dream of traveling the world one day.

Conclusion

I'd like to thank you and congratulate you for transiting my lines from start to finish.

I hope this book was able to help you to understand what is hygge, and how you could apply it to various aspects of your life.

The next step is to assess your current situation, and figure out how you could make it more hyggelig through the lessons you have learned from this book.

To help you through this process, here are the most important things that you should keep in mind while you are evaluating your life:

- The history of hygge shows that how it has been effectively used as a remedy for trying times, and as a way of enhancing one's resilience and endurance.

  Reflect upon the challenges that you are facing now. Write them down, if you wish to do so as well. Then, think of how the core values of hygge—comfort, companionship, relaxation, connection to nature, simplicity, and authenticity—could help you overcome them.

Once you have something in mind, make it your goal to gradually but steadily act upon them in order to turn things around for you.

- Take the time to observe and note the positive changes in your body, mind, spirit, and relationships that have been brought about by the practice of hygge.

  By doing so, you would be able to express gratitude as well, and ultimately gain a better appreciation of the people and things that you have in your life.

- Transform your home into a hyggelig retreat by following the suggestions given in this book. Your main goal when decorating your house is to create an ambience that inspires joyful and warm feelings.

  Remember though to keep things simple, and to stay within your budget. A luxurious house is not automatically hyggelig if you do not feel happy and at ease while staying in it.

- Try your hand at recreating the hyggelig recipes in your own kitchen. You can do so much more with these dishes other than serving them to your family during dinner.

Pack them into nifty containers, and bring them to work as your lunch for the day. Stun your friends by making these as your contribution for potluck parties. Remember, as the saying goes, "The only limit is your imagination."

- Teach your kids the values of hyggelig living by following the recommended parenting strategies of this book. Show them how honesty may be expressed in everything they do and say. Demonstrate to them how to have fun with others without having to rely on expensive trips or gadgets. Allow them to play and pursue their interests without being judged. And most importantly, guide them into becoming highly empathic individuals.

  When carried out in the right manner, these methods could inspire children to continue the same practices to the succeeding generations.

- Create a hyggelig environment for your co-workers, your employees, or yourself by taking inspirations from your home when setting up your workstation, improving the way you work and spend your break time, and fostering good relationships with the people you work with.

- Make it a point to practice hygge even when it is not wintertime. Though the cold season is the peak of hyggelig activities, you know by now that this would not prevent you from feeling happy, warm, relaxed, and connected with the people around you and nature all year round.

As exhibited by the examples shared to you in this book, hygge transcends not just geographical boundaries and cultures, but also the seasons of the year. Therefore, you may be able to create special moments with your loved ones wherever and whenever you want.

- Lead a frugal life by exemplifying the core values of hygge. Through this kind of lifestyle, you would be able to retain—or even improve—the quality of your living without having to spend so much of your resources.

Rather than aiming for quantity, go for a commensurate value for your money instead. Learn new skills that can be useful for a variety of situations. Most importantly, place greater importance on your personal experiences and relationships with other people, and you would surely feel the difference that hygge could bring into your life.

By now, you have gained a solid understanding of hygge—its foundations, teachings, and benefits for your physical health, mental resilience, and emotional stability. You have also learned how hygge improves the way you form new relationships, and improve your current ones.

Aside from the people around you, hygge also encourages you to connect with your surroundings. Your home should be where you feel at ease the most. The way you decorate and arrange it must not be influenced solely by current trends, but rather your personal preferences.

Beyond the home, hygge living involves connecting with nature on a deep level as well. Spend time outside with your family and friends by playing outdoor games and activities. Most importantly, appreciate what nature has to offer without somehow ruining it in the process.

Hygge is intimate, and its expression tend to be unique from one person to another. As such, you should use the examples and suggestions given in this book as reference, not as rules that must be absolutely followed. These are guidelines that you can alter and enhance in order to suit your wants and the demands of your life.

At some point in the future, you might encounter a situation that has not been discussed in this book. If you are uncertain about how you could apply the principles of hygge during that time, just try to recall and follow this simple yet important lesson about living a happy life like a Danish: Slow down, and enjoy each passing moment.

Once again, thank you for selecting this book, and taking the time to read through its content. Ultimately, I hope that you find the hyggelig way of living as a worthwhile pursuit after learning the secrets of the Danish people when it comes living a rewarding, meaningful, and happy life.

I wish you the best of luck!

Printed in Great Britain
by Amazon

50926304R00109